PLANET KASPER

COMIX & TRAGIX
PETER SCHUMANN

Fomite
Burlington, VT

ISBN-13: 978-0-9832063-4-5

Library of Congress Control Number: 2011943601

Fomite
58 Peru Street
Burlington, VT 05401
www.fomitepress.com

TABLE OF CONTENTS

Introduction

The British call him Punch, the Italians, Pulchinello, the Russians, Petruchka, the Native Americans, Coyote. These are the figures we may know. But every culture that worships authority will breed a Punch-like, anti-authoritan resister. Yin and yang -- it has to happen. The Germans call him Kasper.

Truth-telling and serious pranking are dangerous professions when going up against power. Bradley Manning sits naked in solitary; Julian Assange is pursued by Interpol, Obama's Department of Justice, and Amazon.com. But -- in contrast to merely human faces -- masks and theater can often slip through the bars.

Consider our American Kaspers: Charlie Chaplin, Woody Guthrie, Abby Hoffman, the Yes Men -- theater people all, utilizing various forms to seed critique. Their profiles and tactics have evolved along with those of their enemies.

Who are the bad guys that call forth the Kaspers? Over the last half century, with his Bread & Puppet Theater, Peter Schumann has been tireless in naming them, excoriating them with Kasperdom.

****

An early, iconic Schumann naming of the perps occurs at the end of Bread & Puppet's mid-60s Christmas Story:

After the news spreads of Jesus's birth, King Herod picks up the phone:

"Hello, Third Army? Go straight to Bethlehem and kill all the children."

In the next scene a large soldier marches in, in full battle array, and knocks on the door of a tiny puppet house.

"Good evening, Ma'am. Do you happen to have any children in the house?"

"Oh, yes, of course," the little hand-puppet says. "Hansie and Mariechen."

"Can you bring them out, please?"

"Oh certainly, Sergeant. But...why?

"We want to kill them."

"Oh."

The mother then tells the sergeant an amazing story that he'll "never believe, but..." about how the children were just taking a bath and then -- by accident -- they were washed down the drain. The sergeant, stupefied, weeps.

"Oh, lady, that's really terrible. Allow me to extend the condolences of the entire Third Army."

He marches off to the next house where he finds that the six children happened to have just marched off six weeks ago and haven't come back yet.

"Men, King Herod isn't going to be too pleased about this."

The next house turns out to be the Bethlehem Nursery, "And we have 55 sweet, little darlings fast asleep in their sweet little beddy-byes," says the Nurse out her window, "AND YOU GORILLAS ARE WAKING THEM UP WITH YOUR SCREAMING. You better go play soldier somewhere else, or I'll call the authorities."

"Lady," says the sergeant, "we are the authorities."

There's the key. Who is the enemy that must call forth the

Kaspers? The men and ideas that people must turn to for help --
the authorities themselves.

For a while at Bread & Puppet, they were portrayed as "the
Butchers" -- figures in black suits and little black hats. White
faces with no eyes. They did bad things like kill white horses, and
had to be overcome.

They had what Schumann called rotten ideas, and it is later with
the Rotten Idea Theater Company that their plans are comically
and often presented. And who presents them? Kaspers! Four-
foot grotesque masks on five to six foot bodies, tiny legs under
them scurrying around, great foam-rubber slapstick clubs,
swinging, reducing all to chaos.

A brilliant satirical, even obvious, strategy -- to present social/
political norms with the most abnormal faces. If the mask fits,
wear it.

So Kasper wakes again in contemporary America, needed,
perhaps, as never before. His current playground is Glover,
Vermont, a town of a thousand in the Northeast Kingdom of
Vermont. His current birth- and nursing-place is in the
heartmindhands of Peter Schumann.

****

In this volume you have a graphic Kasperdom, a comic book
presenting a comic but serious character in comic but dead-
serious circumstances. Who are the bad guys in Planet Kasper?
The intelligent smooth machinists of capitalism and its
"responsible" lifestyle. That is, the powerful of Western
"Civilization".

Gandhi, when asked what he thought of Western Civilization,
famously replied, "I think it would be a good idea."

Schumann's critique is far more radical, imbued with a modern understanding of the results of Faustian striving. In Planet Kasper, he extols some very non-rotten ideas as alternatives: embracing the unbusiness, great beauty and mysterious nonsense of the naked universe. A life dedicated to non-acceptance of garbage society values.

What does Peter Schumann think of western civilization? Read this book.

****

Western civilization has small purchase on life at Glover. Yes, though they grow much of their own, the puppeteers must buy some food in stores. They must put gas in their touring vehicles. Beyond that, "modern" life is minimal -- the Schumanns have no computer, and if they did, they couldn't really do much with no broadband available. Cell phones don't work. During the summer a hundred people live in tents and shit in outhouses. And though there are no reviews, and no advertising, thousands come to see and applaud them. The entrance fee is zero.

But the cost to spectators is high. While most are already disposed to Peter Schumann's Bread & Puppet critique, they, unlike the puppeteers, must drive back home to cognitive dissonance and highlighted, admitted contradictions.

You can read your copy of Planet Kasper for chuckles. You can read it for a further glimpse into the head of that guy on the back cover blowing two horns. Or you can take it seriously -- as seriously as your life will permit. Or you can change your life.

It's that kind of a book.

Marc Estrin
Burlington, Vermont, 2011
as the power plants of western civilization burn and spew.

BREAD & PUPPET

KASPER 1

CHAPTER ONE

IN WHICH KASPER
CANNOT BE FOUND
BECAUSE HE IS ASLEEP
AND HOW HE FINALLY
WAKES UP GLORIOUSLY

WHERE IS KASPER?
SAID THE PEOPLE

AND THE
BUMBELBEES

WHERE?

ASKED THE PHILOSOPHER

SAID THE
SPARROWS

SAID THE
DONKEY

IS HE POOPING?

IS HE FAR
AWAY?

IS HE GONE
FOR GOOD?

THE FACT THAT NOBODY KNOWS WHERE HE IS OR EVEN WHAT HE IS, IS GOOD FOR HIM. KASPER WHO IS ONLY KASPER WHO IS MOSTLY NOT SEEN AND WHOSE WHEREABOUTS ARE UNCERTAIN IS UNCERTAIN HIMSELF! BUT BECAUSE HE IS UP TO SO MUCH, HIS UNCERTAINTY SERVES HIM WELL

GOOD SPEECH!

HOORAH!

HOORAH!

BUT LOOK!

THE UP-TO-SO-MUCH!

IS FAST ASLEEP

BIRDS VISIT HIM

WAKE UP!

WAKE UP!

NORMAL BIRD

CRAZY BIRD

5

CASPER
A SOLID
SLEEPER

A TOTALLY
CONVINCED
SLEEPER

NO!

THE SMOOTH MACHINES OF THE SMOOTH MACHINE LIFE ROLL OVER HIM BUT HE SLEEPS

6

THE WAR MARCHES OVER HIM BUT HE SLEEPS

BUT KASPER SLEEPS

HIS MOTHER COOKS A VERY GOOD STEW

AND THE WOLVES

AND THE TOADS

THEY FOLLOW THE SMELL OF THE STEW

GLORIOUSLY

BUT THEN THE SUN RISES

7

HE SNIFFS
THE AIR

HE PRICKS UP
HIS EARS

AND HE SAYS
TO HIMSELF

"AND THEN KASPER JUMPED UP LIKE A CANONBALL

AND HE GRABBED HIS CYMBALS!"

CHAPTER TWO

IN WHICH KASPER PREACHES WITH ALL HIS MIGHT ✧ IS BURIED IN ROTTEN TOMATOES BUT SURVIVES TO CONTINUE HIS SERMON

LISTEN TO ME!. I AM KASPER THE SLEEPER AND I DIDN'T WAKE UP DUTIFULLY LIKE I WAS SUPPOSED TO AND THE WAR WENT OVER ME BUT I SLEPT AND THE SMOOTH MACHINE OF THE SMOOTH MACHINELIFE WENT OVER ME BUT I SLEPT AND THE VERY GOOD STEW SMELLED UP OUR HOUSE BUT I SLEPT AND MY SLEEP WAS PERFECT AND NOTHING WAS MISSING IN IT AND MY SLEEPY EYES LOOKED INSIDE AND THE INSIDE IS ALMOST THE SAME AS THE OUTSIDE MINUS THE BULLSHIT AND BECAUSE THE BULLSHIT IS MISSING IT IS GLORIOUS AND THERE IS NO NEED TO WAKE UP UNTIL THE SUN RISES FURIOUSLY AND THEN THE FURY OF THE SUN GETS IN MY THROAT AND I YELL : GET UP FEET!. GET UP EYES ! GET UP BRAIN !

RRR!

MAMA MIA!

RRRA

BUT THE TOMATO DEATH IS ONLY A
TEMPORARY DEATH AND KASPER ARISES
AND HE PICKS UP HIS CYMBALS

CHAPTER THREE

IN WHICH KASPER
PRESSES ON BUT GETS
HIT BY A SNOWSTORM
AND CONSEQUENTLY
ENDS UP WORKING FOR
2 DIFFERENT TYPES OF
FUNERAL BUSINESSES

BUT THE world
is BIG

AND KASPER
IS LITTLE

AND SO HE
DECIDED TO
GO ON

AND ON

TO NOT STOP
ANYWHERE
PARTICULAR

BUT TO PRESS
ON

AND TO FORGET
ALL TOMATOES

AND ALL
FRYING PANS

BUT TO GO ON

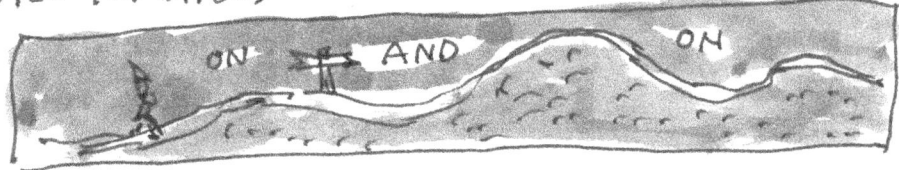

ON   AND   ON

BUT ONE FINE DAY
HE SAYS

AND HE STOPS
GOING ON AND ON

AND HE SITS
DOWN AND SAYS

AND HE SKIS
HIS HEART OUT

18

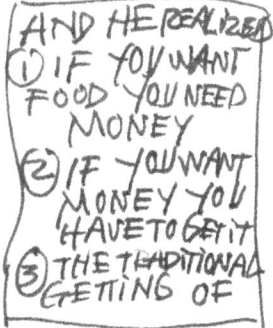

17
But the FUNERALS FOR THINGS AND IDEAS THAT NEED TO BE BURIED ARE SO MANY
PATRIOTISM
B52
NATION BUILDING
KASPER CAN'T FIND TIME FOR THE PRACTISE OF HAPPINESS FOR NO REASON
AND INSTEAD OF REJOICING
HOORAH!
MONEY
OVER THE BURIAL OF SO MANY DECEASED OR ROTTEN IDEAS
MORE
MORE
MORE
KASPER CRIES
BECAUSE HIS JOB NEVER ENDS
AND THE GRAVES ARE NOT DEEP ENOUGH
HE DIGS AND HE DIGS
BUT THE ROTTEN IDEAS KEEP COMING BACK UP
MORE
MONEY
BAD
EVIL
ROTTEN
HORRIBLE
TERRIBLE
NASTY
LOUSY
OH!

CHAPTER FOUR

IN WHICH YOU ENCOUNTER KASPER AS A THINKER AND THE RESULTS OF HIS THINKING TESTIFYING TO HIS RESILIENCE.

AND HE THINKS

THINK

BREAD & PUPPET

KASPER 2

KASPER HAS A NIGHTMARE

AH!

HE RIDES AS FAST AS HE CAN

HE KNOCKS AT THE DOOR

HE SNEAKS IN THROUGH THE BACK DOOR

MRS. WOJCIK IS UP BEFORE DAWN

MILKING

SCYTHING WHEAT

MILLING FLOUR

BAKING BREAD

UNCLE FATSO
PAYS HER A VISIT

39

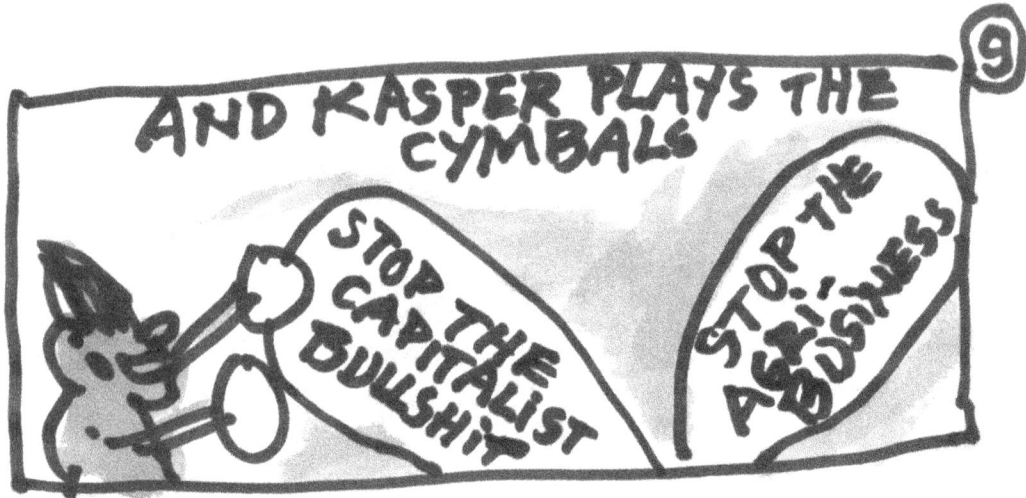

BREAD&PUPPET
PRESS
2002
GLOVER · VT

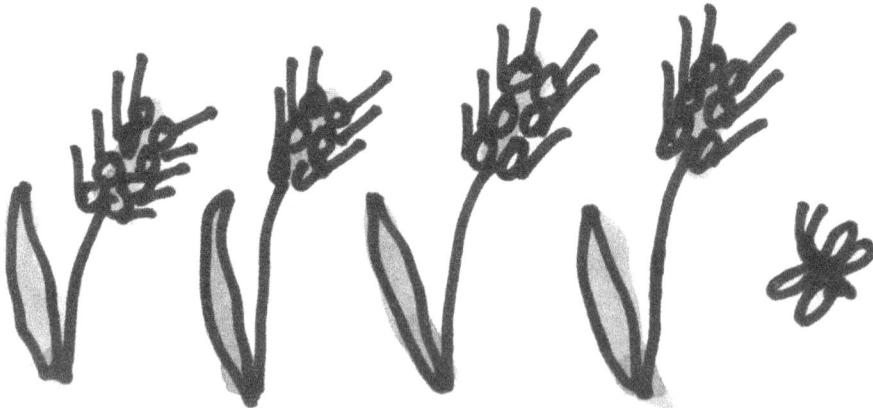

BREAD & PUPPET

KASPER 3

50

CHAPTER TWO

KASPER IN HELL

HELL IS JUNK OR
UNPROCESSED GARBAGE
IN THE HEAD
INHERITED
FROM
THE
GARBAGE
SOCIETY

MY UNFINISHED OR NOT
BUSINESS MY DOINGS
DOINGS
THE MELANCHOLY
OF THE POWERLESS
DOODLES

WHAT THE MAKER THINKS
IS THE MAKING. THE
MAKING'S SENSE IS DIRECTLY
FROM THE WHOLE WORLD.

THE WHOLE WORLD IS BOTH THE GLORY
OF THE WORLD AND THE WRONG WORLD

(3)

WE ARE THE OBVIOUS
RESULTS OF GOVERNMENTS
AND PARENTS. BUT
UNDERNEATH THE
OBVIOUS RESULTS ARE
THE REBELLIOUS
RESULTS

THE CULTIVATION OF NON-ACCEPTANCE
NON-ACCEPTANCE OF WHAT RAINS
DOWN ON US AS NECESSITY OR WHAT
CLAIMS ULTIMATE REALITY

THE MERCHANT REALITY OR THE
LIFE STYLE OF THE RICH AND FAMOUS
DISHED OUT IN PLASTIC FORM TO THE NOT RICH
AND NOT FAMOUS

(4)

I MUST GET
OUT OF HERE

I MUST GET
TO THE POINT

WHERE IS THE
POINT

I MUST FIND
MY CYMBALS

WHERE ARE
MY CYMBALS?

GET OUT OF HERE

GET GOING

58

THE END

BREAD & PUPPET
PRESS · 2002
GLOVER VT.

60

BREAD & PUPPET

KASPER 4

CHAPTER ONE

IN WHICH CASPER WEINBERGER LECTURES KASPER

KASPER VISITS HIS UNCLE CASPER WEINBERGER FORMER US SECRETARY OF DEFENSE

HI CASPER

HI CASPER

NATO AND EU VERY GOOD! POLISH AGRICULTURE VERY BAD!

UH

THE PROBLEM IS HOW TO GET RID OF THE SUPERFLUOUS RURAL POPULATION

BY EXPANDING POLISH CITIES

HOW TO REMOVE INDIVIDUALS FROM THEIR PRESENT COMMUNITIES AND PLACE THEM IN CITIES

AND PLACE THEM IN CITIES WHERE LABOR ETHICS AND ATTITUDES OF ADVANCEMENT ARE BETTER ESTABLISHED

THERE IS REALLY NO LIMIT TO HOW MUCH THE POLISH FARMER WILL DENIGRATE HIS FAMILY TO MAINTAIN HIS LIFESTYLE

HI HO!

HI HO!

PERSONAL FREEDOM BECOMES MORE IMPORTANT AND VALUED IN SUCH A SOCIETY THAN MATERIAL WEALTH!

MAMA MIA!

IN THE U.S. AND EUROPE PEOPLE WHO PRACTICE PERSONAL FREEDOM ABOVE ALL ELSE END UP LIVING UNDER BRIDGES AND ARE GENERALLY SHUNNED BY SOCIETY. IN POLAND THEY HAVE A FAMILY, A DOG AND 10 ACRES OF LAND

OH!

THE ENTIRE CAPITALIST AND RESPONSIBLE LIFESTYLE THAT IS CATCHING ON IN THE BIG CITIES OF POLAND IS THREATENING TO RURAL INDIVIDUALS WHO ARE ACCUSTOMED TO A HAPHAZARD DEVIL-MAY-CARE ATTITUDE TOWARDS MONEY AND LIFE IN GENERAL

ACH!

TO THE CITY!

JUST A MINUTE! I AM LEWIS MUMFORD. LISTEN TO WHAT I HAVE TO SAY ABOUT THE CITY! THE CITY, IN ITS FINAL STAGE OF DEVELOPMENT, BECOMES A COLLECTIVE CONTRIVANCE FOR MAKING THIS IRRATIONAL SYSTEM WORK AND FOR GIVING THOSE WHO ARE IN REALITY ITS VICTIMS

THE ILLUSION OF POWER, WEALTH AND FELICITY, OF STANDING AT THE VERY PINNACLE OF HUMAN ACHIEVEMENT. BUT IN ACTUAL FACT THEIR LIVES ARE CONSTANTLY IN PERIL, THEIR WEALTH IS TASTELESS AND EPHEMERAL, THEIR LEISURE IS SENSATIONALLY MONOTONOUS AND THEIR PATHETIC FELICITY IS TAINTED BY CONSTANT WELL-JUSTIFIED ANTICIPATIONS OF VIOLENCE AND SUDDEN

DEATH. INCREASINGLY THEY FIND THEMSELVES "STRANGERS AND AFRAID" IN A WORLD THEY NEVER MADE: A WORLD EVER LESS RESPONSIVE TO DIRECT HUMAN COMMAND, EVER MORE EMPTY OF HUMAN MEANING.

THANK YOU MR. MUMFORD

YOU ARE WELCOME

BYE KASPER, I HAVE TO GO AND ADVISE THE U.S. ON SOME MORE DEFENSE SPENDING

SO LONG UNCLE

THE CAPITALIST RESPONSIBLE LIFESTYLE

CHAPTER TWO

BUT KASPER TAKES ADVICE FROM LEWIS MUMFORD AND

AND THEN THE BIG BEAST IN WHOSE BELLY KASPER LIVES BELCHES

BELCH

AND PUKES

④

AND MANY KASPERS

POUR ALL OVER THE PLACE

THE END

73

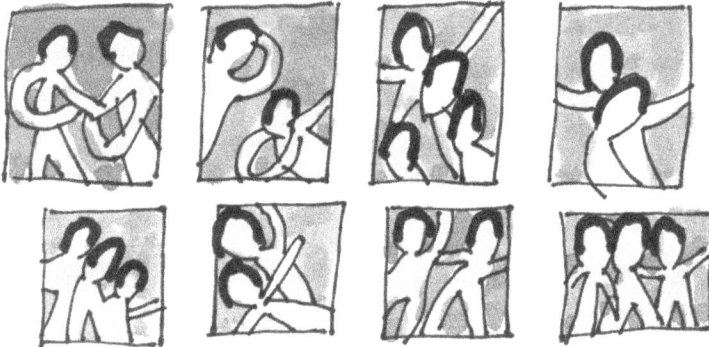

BREAD & PUPPET
PRESS · 2002
GLOVER · VT.

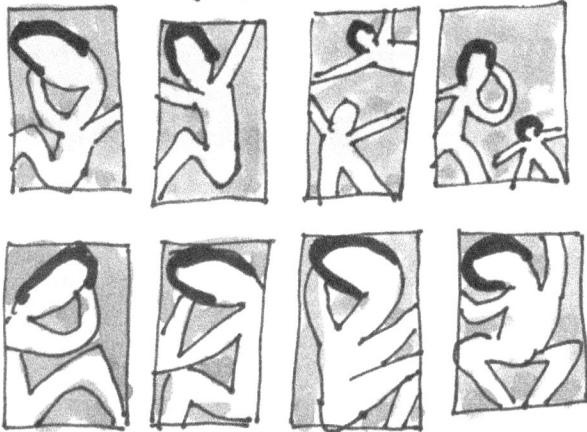

74

BREAD & PUPPET

KASPER 5

FROM HIS
ROTTEN IDEA COLLECTION
HERE ARE SOME OF
KASPERS FINEST
ROTTEN IDEAS

AH!

THE 1ST ROTTEN
IDEA IS CALLED:
CHICKENS

THE EARTH WITHOUT CIVILIZATION IS SO GREAT IT FRIGHTENS US INTO THE ACT OF CIVILIZING. THE WALLS AND ROADS WHICH DIVIDE US FROM THE EARTH INTO AN ENTITY OF OUR OWN ARE PROTESTS AGAINST OUR FEAR. BUT THE DEATH OF OUR PARENTS AND OUR OWN CAR-ACCIDENTS OPEN OUR SMALL ENTITY TO THE GIANT ENTITY OF THE EARTH. IN OTHER WORDS: WE NEVER SUCCEED WITH OUR OWN ROAD + WALL ENTITY WHICH WE CALL CIVILIZATION. OUR PICTURES MIRROR DEATH. OUR MUSIC BABBLES LIKE DEATH AND OUR LANGUAGE PUSHES ITS TERMS CONTINUOUSLY AWAY FROM OURSELVES AND TOWARDS THE EARTH WHICH INCLUDES DEATH.

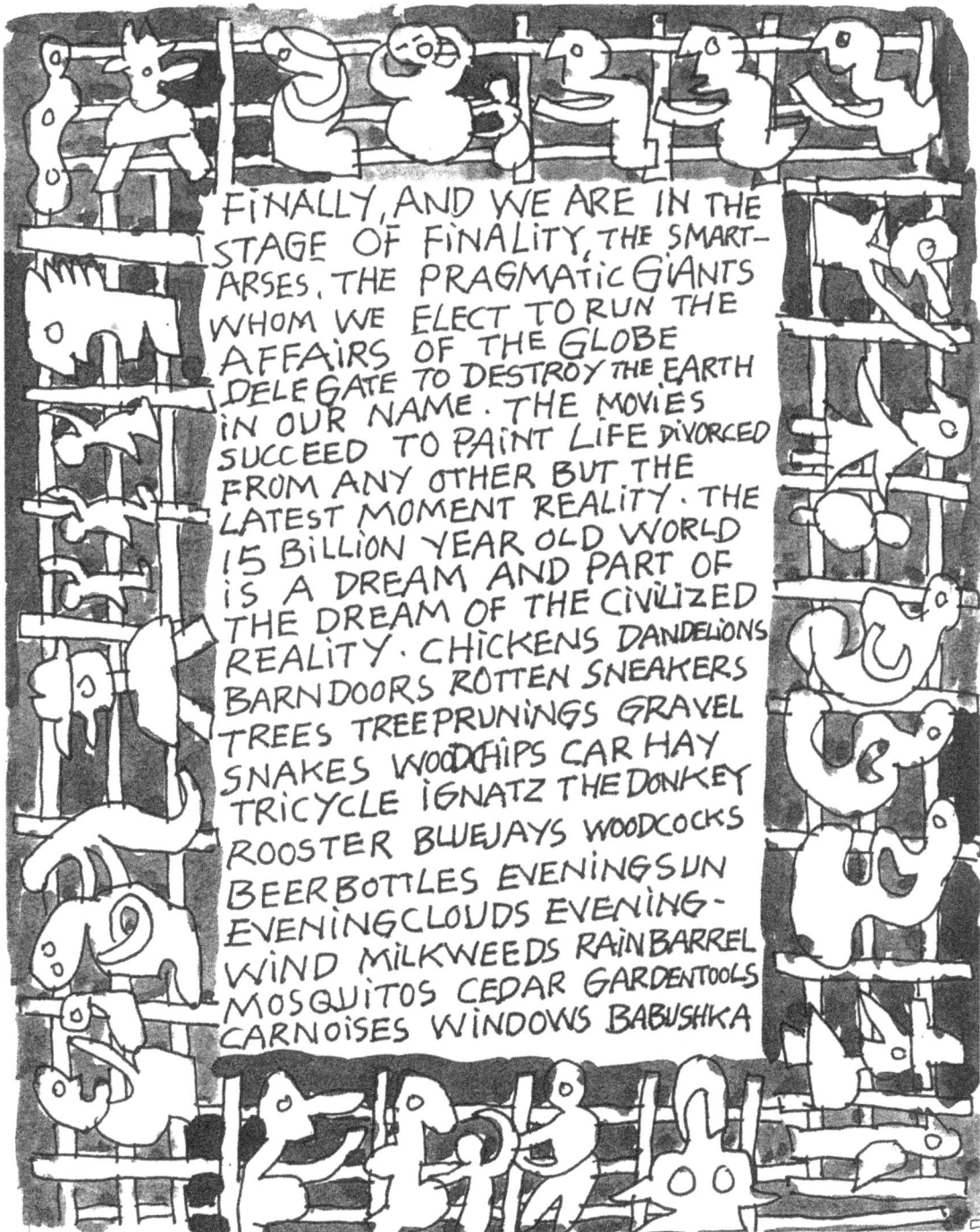

FINALLY, AND WE ARE IN THE STAGE OF FINALITY, THE SMART-ARSES, THE PRAGMATIC GIANTS WHOM WE ELECT TO RUN THE AFFAIRS OF THE GLOBE DELEGATE TO DESTROY THE EARTH IN OUR NAME. THE MOVIES SUCCEED TO PAINT LIFE DIVORCED FROM ANY OTHER BUT THE LATEST MOMENT REALITY. THE 15 BILLION YEAR OLD WORLD IS A DREAM AND PART OF THE DREAM OF THE CIVILIZED REALITY. CHICKENS DANDELIONS BARNDOORS ROTTEN SNEAKERS TREES TREEPRUNINGS GRAVEL SNAKES WOODCHIPS CAR HAY TRICYCLE IGNATZ THE DONKEY ROOSTER BLUEJAYS WOODCOCKS BEERBOTTLES EVENINGSUN EVENINGCLOUDS EVENING-WIND MILKWEEDS RAINBARREL MOSQUITOS CEDAR GARDENTOOLS CARNOISES WINDOWS BABUSHKA

THE 2ND ROTTEN
IDEA IS CALLED:
SOUP

REVOLUTION IS PRECEDED BY
CULTURAL REVOLUTION. THE
MINDS OF THE MONEY EATERS
ARE PAPERMACHÉ. THEREFORE
PAPERMACHÉ ATTACKS THEM.
THE OWNERS OF PROSPERITY
ARE THE EARTHMUTILATORS
AND URBANIZERS URBANIZING
AGRICULTURE AND WILDERNESS.
THE NON-OWNERS OF PROSPERITY
ARE THE MIDGETS OF CIVILIZATION.
THEY TAKE THE WORDS OUT OF
THE MOUTH OF PROSPERITY
AND TRANSFORM THEM INTO
ATTACK. WE THE MIDGETS
OF THE MONEYWORLD MAKE
MONEY SOUP AND MONEY POOP.

THE MIDGETS SING: NOTHING IS
FOREVER NOT EVEN MONEY+POOP.
THE CRAZINESS OF THE WORLD
IS IN US BECAUSE THE WORLD
IS COMPOSED OF GIANT CHUNKS
OF CRAZINESS MIXED WITH A
REALITY THAT SMELLS+BLOSSOMS
+ IS REAL. THE REALITY OF THE
MONEYEATERS IS FEEDING
THE WORLD MONEY. THEREFORE
WE INVENTED A SOUP CALLED
MONEYSOUP WHICH MAKES
EXCELLENT STOMACHACHES
WHICH REQUIRE EXCELLENT
MEDICAL SERVICES FOR THE
EXCELLENT OWNERS OF
PROSPERITY POOPERITY
SOUPERITY OWNERERITY
URBANERITY COFFEEHOUSERITY
GLOBALERITY FINALERITY

THE 3RD
ROTTEN IDEA
is CALLED:
OH

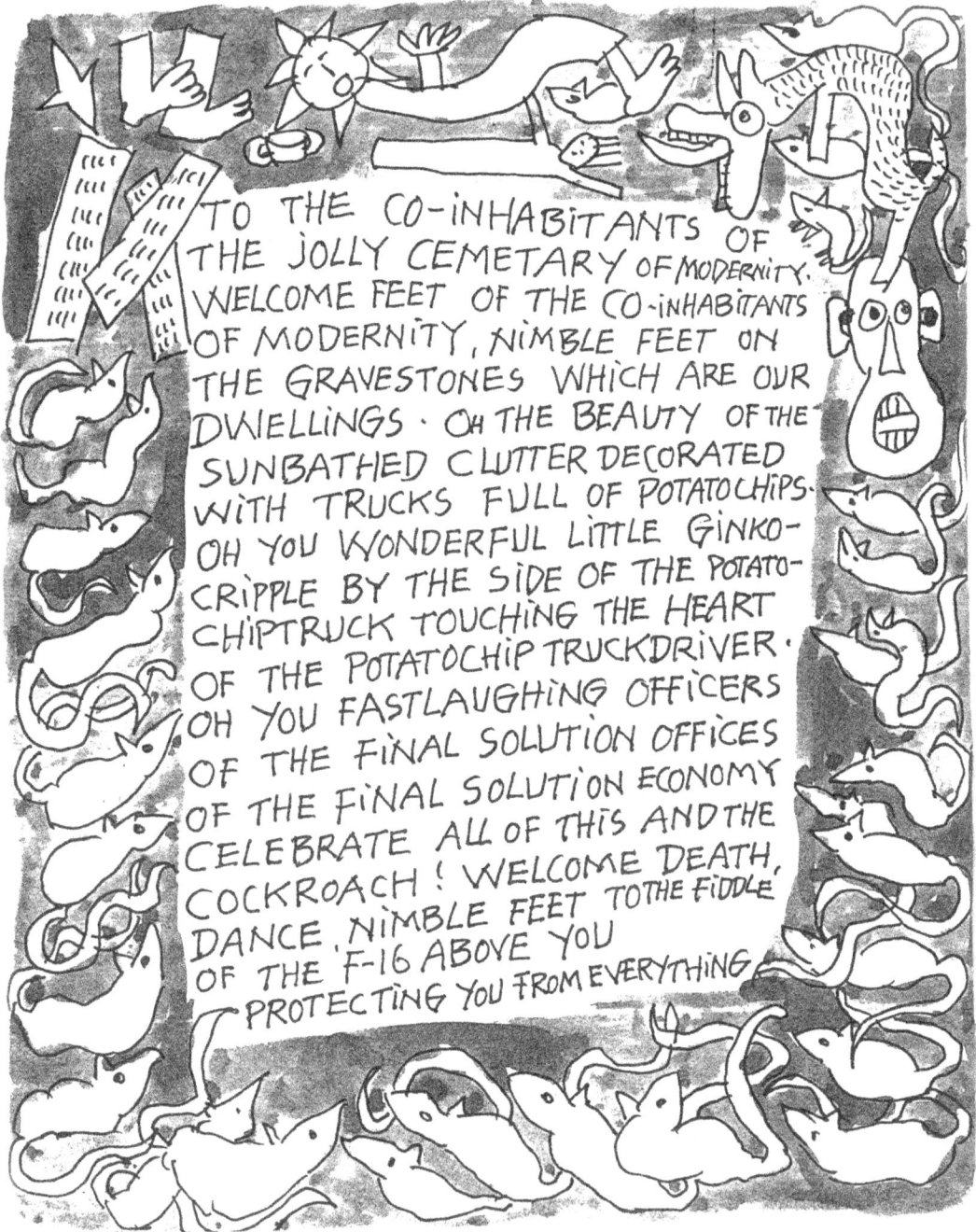

TO THE CO-INHABITANTS OF
THE JOLLY CEMETARY OF MODERNITY.
WELCOME FEET OF THE CO-INHABITANTS
OF MODERNITY, NIMBLE FEET ON
THE GRAVESTONES WHICH ARE OUR
DWELLINGS. OH THE BEAUTY OF THE
SUNBATHED CLUTTER DECORATED
WITH TRUCKS FULL OF POTATOCHIPS.
OH YOU WONDERFUL LITTLE GINKO-
CRIPPLE BY THE SIDE OF THE POTATO-
CHIPTRUCK TOUCHING THE HEART
OF THE POTATOCHIP TRUCKDRIVER.
OH YOU FASTLAUGHING OFFICERS
OF THE FINAL SOLUTION OFFICES
OF THE FINAL SOLUTION ECONOMY
CELEBRATE ALL OF THIS AND THE
COCKROACH! WELCOME DEATH,
DANCE, NIMBLE FEET TO THE FIDDLE
OF THE F-16 ABOVE YOU
PROTECTING YOU FROM EVERYTHING.

THE 4TH
ROTTEN IDEA
IS CALLED:
THE FOOT OF PARADISE

HOW CAN YOU SAY YOU ARE
HAPPY WHEN THE SUBJECT MATTER OF
YOUR METIER IS EXACTLY UNHAPPINESS?
BECAUSE HAPPINESS IS AN ABSENCE OF
PAIN RELATIONSHIP OF BODY + SOUL
EVEN UNDER DIFFICULT OR PAINFUL
CIRCUMSTANCES. THE METIER
MAKES HAPPY. A GREAT TASK
WIDENS THE WORKER. THE UN-
FULLFILLED GREATNESS OF THE
METIER MAKES FOR THE GREAT-
NESS OF COMMITMENT WHICH
HAPPINESS REQUIRES. THE
FULLNESS IN THIS UNFULLFILLED
STATE MAKES THE COMMITTED
WORKER HAPPY. THE
PARADISE SEEKER HAS ONE
FOOT IN PARADISE.
THAT ONE FOOT IS THE
FOOT OF HAPPINESS

THE 5TH
ROTTEN IDEA
IS CALLED:
TOES

AH! EH! OH! UH! WE ARE DYING SO MANY DEATHS EVERY DAY. OUR BORING DEATH LOOKS AT US SO MANY TIMES EVERY DAY. OUR DEATH STINKS LIKE THE SOCKS WHICH ARE THE STRAIGHTJACKETS OF OUR TOES WHO YEARN FOR FREEDOM. OUR TOES WHO FOLLOW THE UTILITARIAN WAYS OF OUR KNEES. OUR KNEES WHO ARE POLITE AND NOT REBELLIOUS AND ARE EDUCATED BY OUR GAIT WHICH IS THE GAIT OF SLAUGHTERHOUSE ANIMALS AND CARRIES US ON THE DESIGNED PATHS. BUT WHAT ARE

THE DESIGNED PATHS? AND WHO
ARE THE DESIGNERS? CITIZENS OF TOES
CITIZENS OF KNEES CITIZENS OF DESIGNED
PATHS LOOK AT THE DESIGNERS! LOOK
AT THEIR TOES LOOK AT THEIR KNEES
WATCH THEIR GAIT! THEY THEMSELVES
ARE DESIGNED BY THE DESIGNS WITH
WHICH THEY FORCE YOUR GAIT IN
THE DIRECTION OF THE SLAUGHTER-
HOUSE. THEY THEMSELVES ARE
DIRECTED TO THE SLAUGHTER-
HOUSE. TASTE THEIR PIE!
LISTEN TO THEIR SONG!
THEIR PIE TASTES LIKE THE LAST
PIE EVER! THEIR SONG IS THE
ETERNAL BYE-BYE SONG. BYE-BYE
BYE BYE BYE BYE BYE BYE
AH! EH! OH! UH! UH! UH!

AND NOW KASPER
THE ROTTEN IDEA COLLECTOR
IS TIRED AND
TAKES
A NAP

BREAD & PUPPET PRESS
2002 GLOVER VT.

BREAD & PUPPET

KASPER 6

ON MONDAY KASPER MEETS THE CHICKENMAN

THE CHICKEN-MAN DIES

KASPER LOOKS

STRAIGHT THROUGH DEATH

INTO A FIELD OF POPPIES

UP! UP!

CRY THE POPPIES

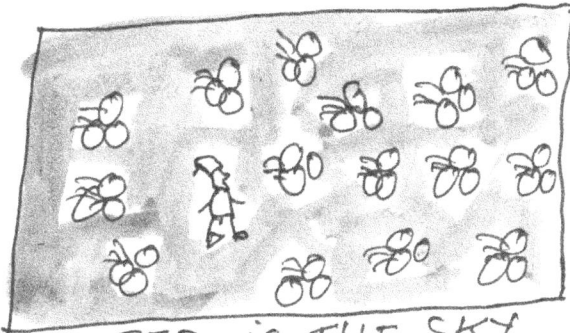

RED IS THE SKY

③

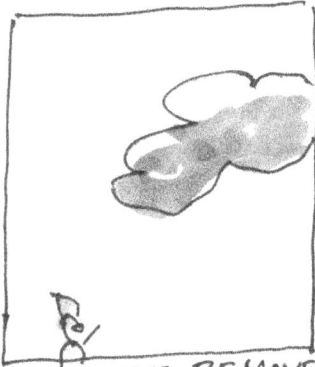

KASPER REMOVES
HIMSELF TO
ANOTHER LOCATION

STEPS INTO
DOGPOOP

TURNS LEFT

TURNS RIGHT

SITS STRAIGHT

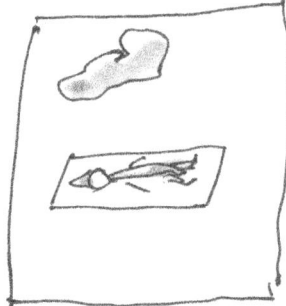

LIES DOWN

KASPER GOES
TO THE HOSPITAL

SPEAKING
TREE LANGUAGE

HE ADDRESSES THE PILLOWS

ARISE AND SHINE!

THE PILLOWS JUMP INTO THE SUNSHINE

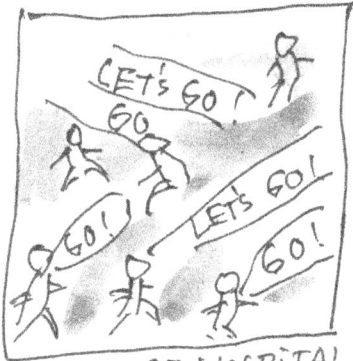

LET'S GO! GO! GO! LET'S GO! GO!

END OF HOSPITAL

GET HIM!

KASPER RUNS AWAY

THE COPS ARE AFTER HIM

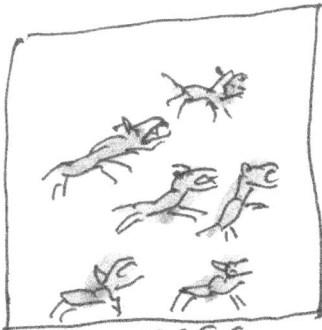

THE DOGS CHASE HIM

KASPER HIDES IN A MOUSEHOLE

I AM IN THE DARK. IN ORDER TO SEE THE LIGHT I NEED TO MAKE MORE DARK THEN IT MIGHT HAPPEN THAT I SEE

WITH MORE & MORE DARK
& LESS & LESS LIGHT KASPER
WATCHES A FEW JOLLY
SPECKS OF DUST REPRESENTATIVES
OF THE 'UNIVERSE

AND HE COMES TO A NUMBER OF CONCLUSIONS ⑥

1.) DON'T BE AFRAID

2) ALWAYS REMEMBER THE POPPIES

3) FOCUS YOUR SPYGLASS ON DEATH

4) WITH MINIMALIST REQUESTS HAVE MAXIMALIST EXPECTATIONS

5) SIT

6) LIE DOWN

7) TURN LEFT

8) TURN RIGHT

9) RUN

10) DON'T RUN

11) SEE, EVEN IF IT'S UNPLEASANT

12) PRODUCE LIGHT EVEN WITHOUT ELECTRICITY

13) MAKE EVERYTHING

14) DON'T STOP

15) NO HURRY

16) MAKE MUSIC FROM THE QUIET IN THE MOUSEHOLE

AND THE MOUSE ASKS

AND KASPER FORMULATES
A FEW ANSWERS TO THE
WHY QUESTION

THE GREAT BEAUTY
OF THE UNIVERSE
MAKES TRIVIAL THE
COPS THE DOGS AND
THE LANDING ON THE
MOON

THE GREAT BEAUTY
OF THE UNIVERSE
IS AVAILABLE
WITHOUT
WAGE SLAVERY
AND THEREFORE
MAKES
WAGE SLAVERY
OBSOLETE

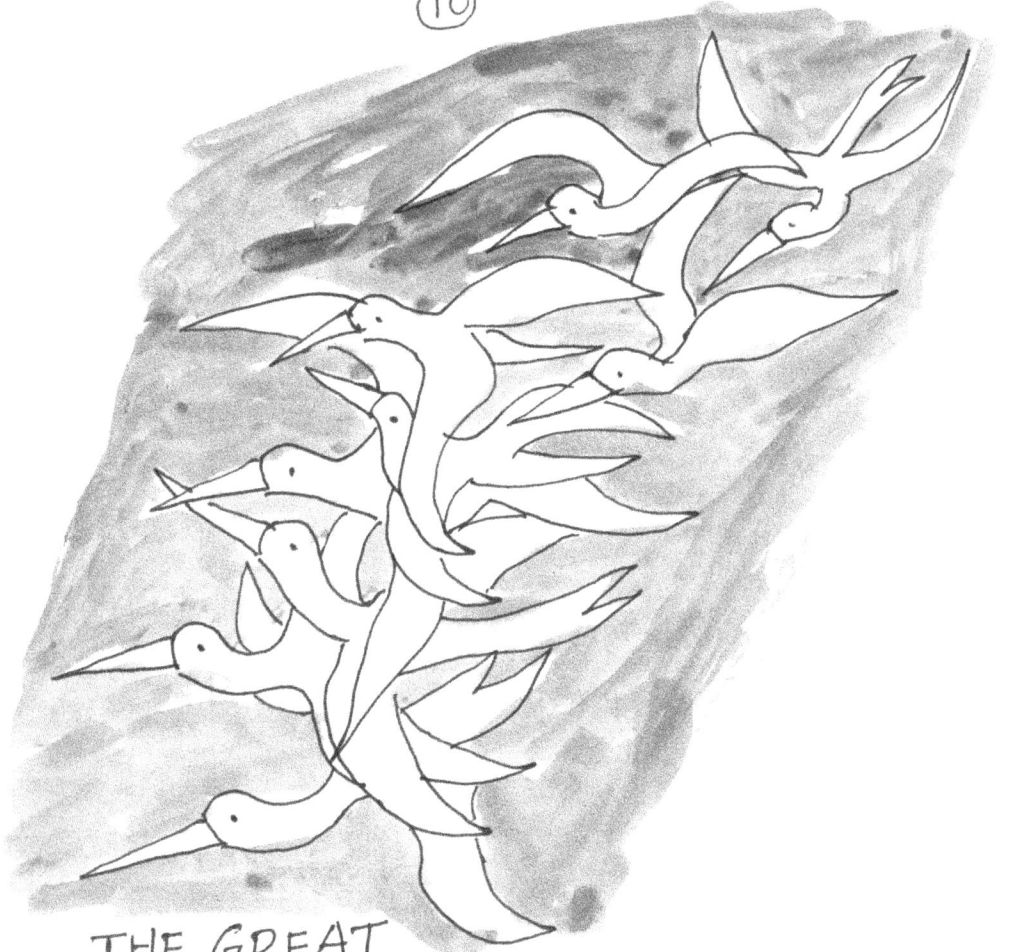

THE GREAT
BEAUTY OF THE UNIVERSE
IS A SKY OR A MUDPUDDLE

THE GREAT
BEAUTY OF THE
UNIVERSE IS NOT
TOURISM THAT SELLS
SKY AND MUDPUDDLE

THE GREAT BEAUTY OF THE UNiiVERSE. SHiTS ON THE IMF

SUCH ARE THE
FORMULATIONS
THAT KASPER
PROVIDED FOR
THE MOUSE

BREAD
&PUPPET
PRESS
2002

BREAD & PUPPET

KASPER 7

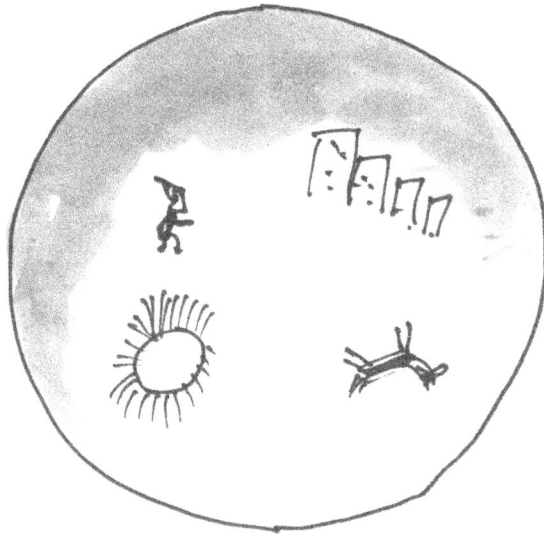

KASPER'S
UNREALITY

KASPER GOES
FISHING

HE IS SWALLOWED
BY A BIG FISH

THE BIG FISH GOES
TO THE DEAD OCEAN

AND DIES THE
DEAD OCEAN DEATH

AT THAT POINT
KASPER GETS
BORN INTO UNREALITY

HE HAS NOTHING BUT HIS GODGIVEN TIME

HE HANDS OVER HIS GODGIVEN TIME + THEY GIVE HIM MONEY

EVERY DAY HE TAKES HIS GODGIVEN TIME + MESSES IT UP

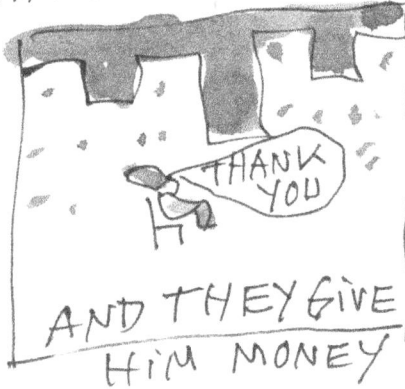

AND THEY GIVE HIM MONEY

BUT THE CAR IS A HEARSE

AND CAN ONLY GO TO THE CEMETARY

AND WHEN IT GETS TO THE CEMETARY

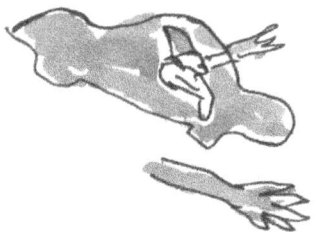

IT KILLS HIS ARM

BUT RATHER THAN MESSING UP HIS GOD-GIVEN TIME KASPER STILL WANTS TO GO SOMEWHERE NICE

AND THIS TIME THE CAR KILLS

HIS FOOT

AND WITHOUT AN ARM AND A FOOT KASPER HAS TO MESS UP HIS GOD GIVEN TIME EVEN MORE

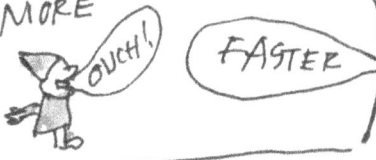

OUCH!

FASTER

AND HE ORDERS HIS CAR TO TAKE HIM REALLY SOMEWHERE REALLY NICE

REALLY NICE

⑤

BUT THIS TIME THE CAR KILLS HIS HEAD

AND KASPER IS UNDONE

AND IS NO KASPER ANYMORE

AND AS NOKASPER HE IS STILL IN UNREALITY

ONLY HE NOW LOOKS LIKE THIS

AND LIKE THIS

AND HE WALKS AROUND FREELY AND INVISIBLY

AND HE CHECKS OUT UNREALITY

AND THEN NOKASPER GETS VERY SICK

FROM SO MUCH UNREALITY

AND HE THINKS HE IS DYING AGAIN

BUT LUCKILY A DOCTOR PASSES BY

AND GIVES HIM A REALITY PILL

AND HE SEES

AND HE SEES
REALITY'S BEAUTY
AND BITTERNESS
AND DEATH

AND THE
CLOUDS ARE
ALIVE AND
LOOK FAMILIAR

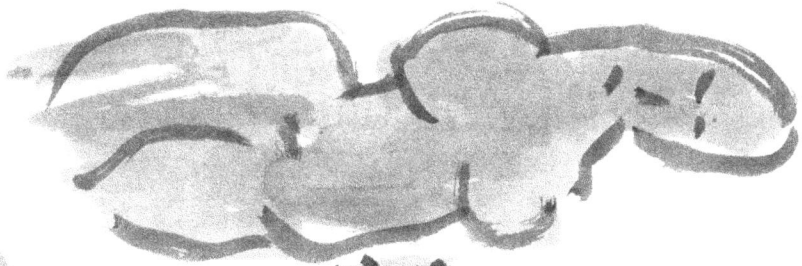

AND KASPER SAYS : i WILL GO BACK TO UNREALITY AND SUBVERT iT WiTH UNBUSINESS, THE BiGGEST, FULL-OF-DEDICATION-UNBUSINESS NOT MARRIED TO REASON OR THE PROFITMOTIV HiDDEN iN REASON

THE UNBUSINESS
OF INSECTS AND
WORMS AND THE
UNBUSINESS OF NONSENSE
AND THE UNBUSINESS
OF SURPLUS POPULATIONS
AND GENERALLY
DISCARDABLE PEOPLE
WHO ARE STICKS
IN THE PATH OF
UPWARD MOBILITY
BECAUSE THEIR
MOBILITY IS CHEAP

AND THEIR DOORS
ARE UNCLOSED &
THEIR DARKNESS IS
UNLIT & THEIR BEER
IS UNDRUNK & THEIR
COCKTAILS ARE NON-
EXISTENT. & THEY
ARE NOT REPRESENTED
BY JETS & THEY KNOW
THAT ALL EMPLOYMENT
STINKS FROM SUFFERING
AND THEY KNOW
THAT MONEY
IS NOT WHAT
IT PRETENDS
TO BE

BREAD& PUPPET
PRESS
2002

BREAD & PUPPET

KASPER 8

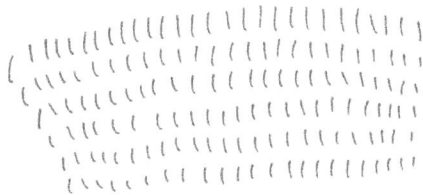

THE ANTI-DEPRESSING KASPER

(SUITED FOR
BIRTHDAYS &
OTHER
THOUGHTFUL
OCCASIONS)

FOR MARIA — 2 TAKE 2 ♡

THERE WERE ANGELS
IN THE SKY

BUT WHEN HE
LOOKED CLOSER
THEY WERE DEVILS

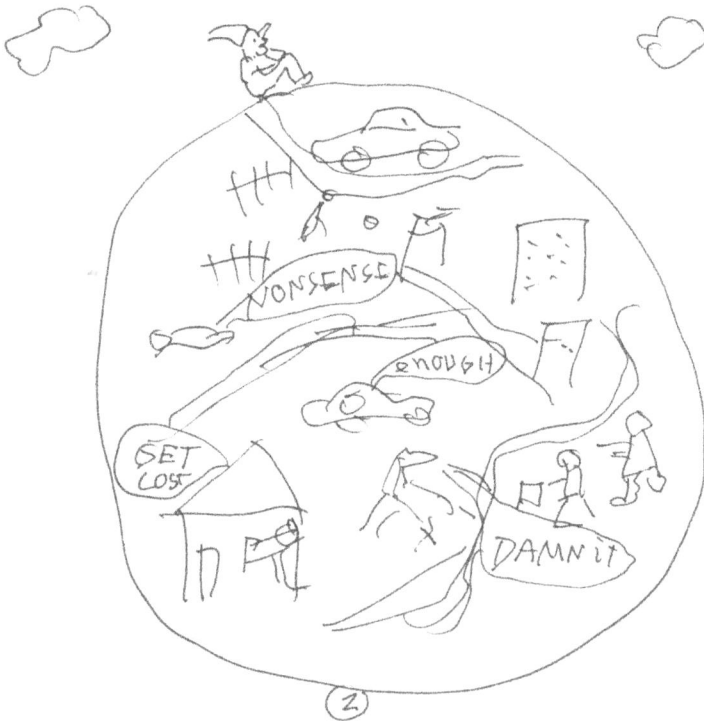

NONSENSE

ENOUGH

GET
LOST

DAMN IT

THE COUNTRY WHERE KASPER LIVED
HAD A SIGN ON IT

FREEDOOM END DEMOCRAZY

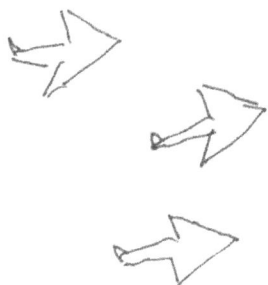

KASPER THREW
ROTTEN EGGS AT
THE SIGN

THAT'S FOR YOU

BUT THE EGGS SPLASHED
BACK ON HIS HEAD
AND HE HAD TO TAKE A BATH

THEN HE MADE A BIG DRAGON TO ATTACK THE SIGN
BUT THE COPS ARRESTED THE DRAGON

4

130

FREEDOOM END DEMOCRAZY

THEN HE TRIED TO

⑤

LUCKILY HE FELL RIGHT INTO HIS OWN BED

(WHICH HIS WIFE HAD HAD THE PRESENCE OF MIND TO PULL UNDER THE SIGN)

AND THE BED WAS GOOD & THE PILLOW WAS FRIENDLY & MADE HIM READ :

HOW CAN WE MAKE THINGS BEAUTIFUL, ATTRACTIVE & DESIRABLE FOR US WHEN THEY ARE NOT? AND I RATHER THINK THAT IN THEMSELVES THEY NEVER ARE. HERE WE COULD LEARN SOMETHING FROM PHYSICIANS WHEN THEY DILUTE WHAT IS BITTER — BUT EVEN MORE FROM ARTISTS WHO ARE REALLY CONTINUALLY TRYING TO BRING OFF SUCH FEATS. MOVING AWAY FROM THINGS UNTIL THERE IS A GOOD DEAL THAT ONE NO LONGER SEES & THERE IS MUCH THAT OUR EYE HAS TO ADD IF WE ARE STILL TO SEE THEM AT ALL; OR TO PLACE THEM SO THAT THEY PARTIALLY CONCEAL EACH OTHER & GRANT US ONLY GLIMPSES OF ARCHITECTURAL PERSPECTIVES OR LOOKING AT THEM THROUGH TINTED GLASS OR IN THE LIGHT OF THE SUNSET, OR GIVING THEM A SURFACE & SKIN THAT IS NOT FULLY TRANSPARENT — ALL THIS WE SHOULD LEARN FROM ARTISTS WHILE BEING WISER THAN THEY ARE IN OTHER MATTERS. FOR WITH THEM THIS SUBTLE POWER USUALLY COMES TO AN END WHERE ART ENDS & LIFE BEGINS, BUT WE WANT TO BE THE POETS OF OUR LIFE — FIRST OF ALL IN THE SMALLEST, MOST EVERYDAY MATTERS.

Nietzsche

WOW HM AH OH AHA

6

132

MORE : THE DANGER OF THE HAPPIEST!

TO HAVE REFINED SENSES INCLUDING THE SENSE OF TASTE, TO BE ACCUSTOMED TO THE MOST EXQUISITE THINGS OF THE SPIRIT AS IF THEY WERE SIMPLY THE RIGHT & MOST CONVENIENT NOURISHMENT, TO ENJOY A STRONG, BOLD, AUDACIOUS SOUL, TO GO THROUGH LIFE WITH A CALM EYE & FIRM STEP, ALWAYS PREPARED TO RISK ALL — FESTIVELY, IMPELLED BY THE LONGING FOR UNDISCOVERED WORLDS & SEAS, PEOPLE & GODS, TO HARKEN TO ALL CHEERFUL MUSIC AS IF IT WERE A SIGN THAT BOLD WOMEN, MEN, SEAFARERS WERE PROBABLY SEEKING THEIR BRIEF REST & PLEASURE THERE & IN THE MOST PROFOUND ENJOYMENT OF THE MOMENT, TO BE OVERCOME BY TEARS & THE WHOLE ⑦

133

CRIMSON MELANCHOLY OF THE HAPPY:
WHO WOULD NOT WISH THAT ALL THIS
MIGHT BE HIS POSSESSION, HIS STATE!
NIETZSCHE

135

BREAD & PUPPET
PRESS 2003
GLOVER VT

BREAD & PUPPET

KASPER 9

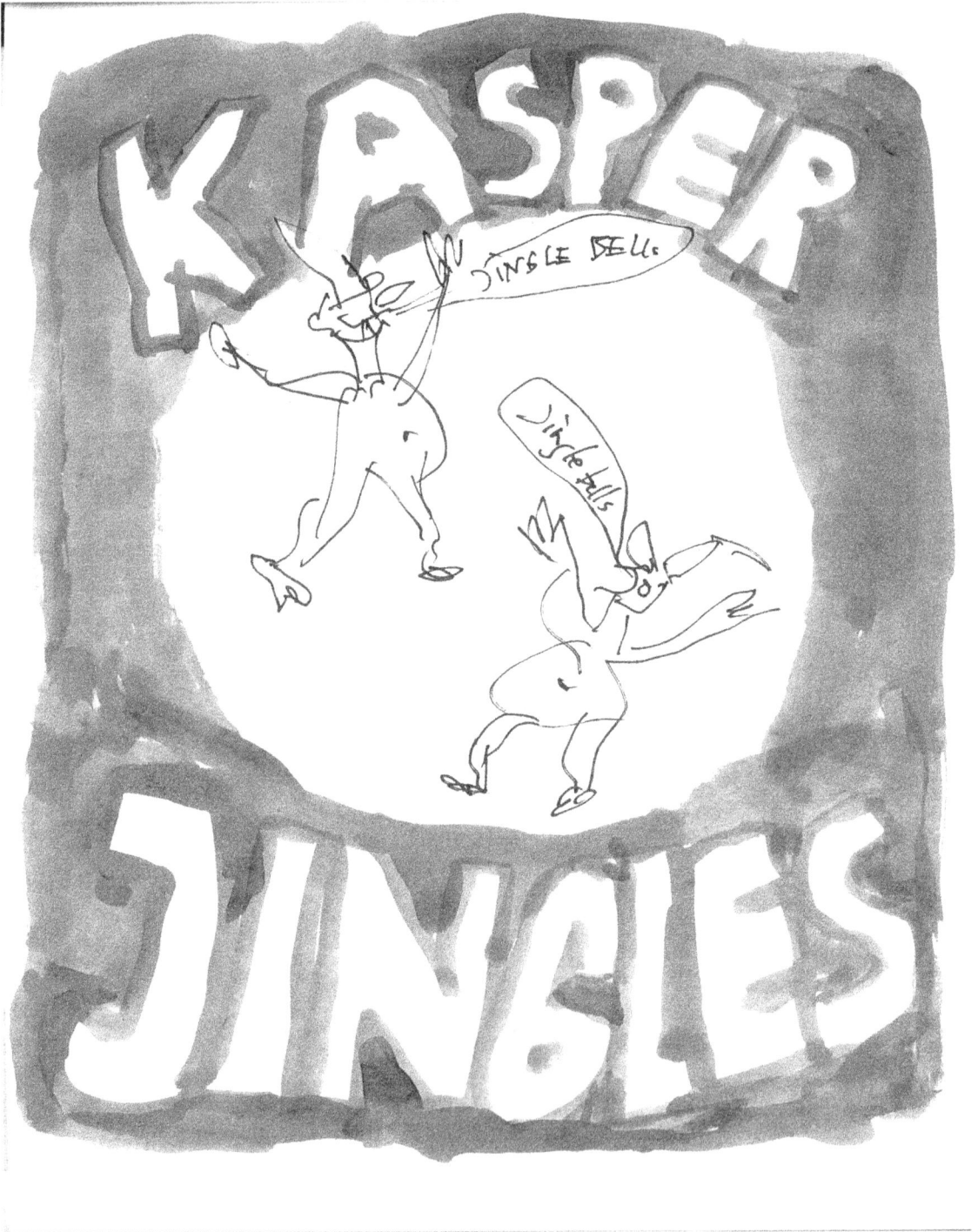

WHEN KASPER LOOKED OUT HIS WINDOW ONE DAY

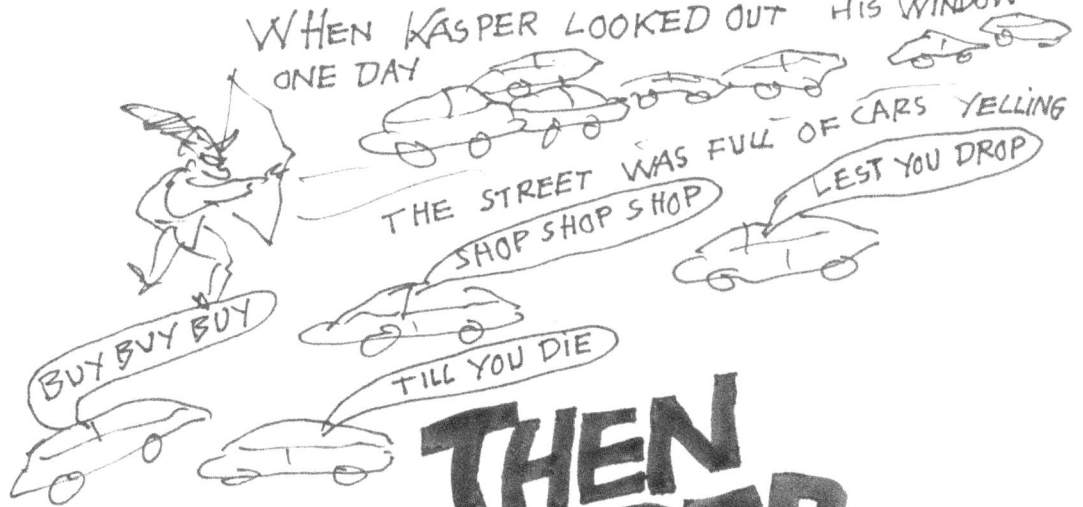

THE STREET WAS FULL OF CARS YELLING

SHOP SHOP SHOP

LEST YOU DROP

BUY BUY BUY

TILL YOU DIE

THEN KASPER

TOOK OFF HIS SHOES & BAREFOOTED TO THE JINGLEMILL & HIS FRIEND THE JINGLEMILLER WAS GLAD TO SEE HIM

HI

LET'S CRANK OUT SOME JINGLES ON THAT OLD JINGLEMILL

YES! LET'S!!

141

STAND UP & BE COUNTED
THE JOLLY TIMES ARE HERE

STAND UP & BE COUNTED
& DRINK A JUG OF BEER

THE UNIVERSE IS MARVELLOUS
IT FLOWS RIGHT TO YOUR SHORE

THE UNIVERSE IS MARVELLOUS
JUST OPEN YOUR DOOR

THE LIGHT WANTS TO SEE YOU
IT'S SHINING IN YOUR EYES

THE LIGHT WANTS TO SEE YOU
I SAY IT TWICE

JUST TAKE A SHOVEL DIG A HOLE & PUT A SHOPPING CENTER IN IT!

LET ME POUR SOME GREASE IN THAT OLD MILL

②

142

O.K.

CRANK AWAY!!

WALMART
GIANT FART
OF CONCRETE
A MILLION SQUARE
FEET

BUY SOME NOTHING
FOR YOUR EVERYTHING
AD SOME SPICE
TO MAKE IT NICE
WHEN YOUR ARSE IS SMART
IT GOES TO WALMART

THE PARADISE
OF THE CHEAPEST PRICE
SELLS THE HELL
OF THE WAY-TOO-WELL
WHAT YOU BUY
IS THE LITTLE GUY
WHOM THEY SQUEEZE
WITH THEIR SLEAZE

THE EARTH WAS NOT SO SMART
GOT MADE INTO A WALMART
ALL ITS PARTS ARE NOW FOR SALE
ALL ITS SALADS LIMP & STALE
ALL ITS JUNGLES FENCED
ALL ITS BEASTS CONDENSED
INTO A SMARTARSE LITTLE SALE
LIMP & STALE

MR. WALMART IS SO FAIR
THAT MAKES HIM A BILLIONAIRE
HE SWALLOWS ALL THE LITTLE GUYS
TO PRODUCE THE CHEAPEST PRICE
HE IS THE KING OF EVERYTHING
WE ARE THE SHEEP
HE'S OUT TO REAP

③

JINGLE MILLER WE NEED **MORE**

OK

TAKE THE LITTLE SHOPPER
PUT HIM IN A CHOPPER
DRESS HIM UP & MAKE HIM FINE
WAIT YOUR TURN & STAND IN LINE
GIVE HIM PLENTY TIME TO THINK
FEED HIM & THEN LET HIM STINK
COME TO THE SHOPPER'S PARADISE
THE SHOPPER IS THE MERCHANDISE

JINGLE BELLS JINGLE BELLS
WALMART'S READY TO COME
GOOD FOR YOUR SYSTEM
GOOD FOR YOUR MOM
IT CHEWS IT UP THE EARTH
IT TURNS IT TO FURNITURE, LIPSTICK & YOU
& GOD IS FURNITURE
JINGLE BELLS JINGLE BELLS
HOW NICE TO HAVE IT ALL
LET'S GET IT QUICKLY BEFORE THE FALL
THE FALL IS SURE TO COME
& THE FALL IS NO GOOD FOR YOUR MOM
FOR YOUR SYSTEM OR YOUR MOM
JINGLE BELLS JINGLE BELLS
HURRY HURRY HURRY
THE BEST THING IS TO STUFF OURSELVES
& NOT TO WORRY

④

144

ON HIS WAY HOME FROM THE JINGLE MILL KASPER NOTICED THAT THE WORLD WAS ON FIRE

⑤

146

147

AND HIS TEETH
STARTED TO JINGLE

AND A TOOTH JINGLE
INTERPRETER WHO WAS
IN THE NEIGHBORHOOD
NOTED DOWN WHAT
THE TEETH JINGLED

As MILK MAKES CHEESE
SO DO BOMBS MAKE PEACE
THE PRESIDENT TELLS THEM
AS HE SHELLS THEM

THE WORLD IS BURNING
DESPITE OUR LEARNING
WE HEAR THE WORLD CRY
AS WE WALK BY

WHEN THE WORLD IS ON FIRE
OUR SOULS ARE FOR HIRE
THEY WATCH ON TV
WHAT THEY SHOULD BE
THEY SIT IN A CHAIR
AS THE WORLD GROWS BARE

THE WORLD IS SOUR & SWEET
THE WORLD IS OUR DAILY MEAT
THE WORLD IS LOW & ALSO HIGH
THE WORLD WEARS OUR SUIT & TIE
WE OWN HER & WE MAKE HER FLY
WE USE HER LIFE & LET HER DIE

9

149

THE STATE OF THE WORLD
is AN ORANGE ALERT
WE ARE GIVEN CHOICE
BUT HAVE NO VOICE
OUR CHOICE IS A MESS
OUR VOICE IS DISTRESS
AS WE WATCH THE WORLD
iN iTS ORANGE ALERT

JiNGLE BELLS jiNGLE BELLS
OH WHAT A FUNNY SiGHT
ALL THE WORLD is UPSiDE-DOWN
& NOTHiNG STANDS UPRiGHT

JiNGLE BELLS jiNGLE BELLS
WHO KNOWS WHAT TO DO
THE PRESiDENT STANDS ON HiS NOSE
& J SiT iN MY SHOE
JiNGLE BELLS JiNGLE BELLS
i DON'T TRUST WHAT i SEE
THE SHARKS DRiVE ON THE HiGHWAY
THE CARS SWiM iN THE SEA
JiNGLE BELLS JiNGLE BELLS
THiS WORLD MUST STOP RiGHT NOW
THE GOVERNMENT PRODUCES MILK
WE ARE iTS HOLY COW
JiNGLE BELLS JiNGLE BELLS
THE MiLK TRANSFORMS TO CHEESE
LEARN FROM THE FERMENTATION
& REBEL PLEASE!

WHEN THE WORLD iS ON FiRE
WE CLiMB EVEN HiRE
WHO KNOWS WHY
WE WANT THE SKY

WE iNHERiT THE EARTH
WiTH OUR BiRTH
WE DRiNK HER UP
iN A PRETTY CUP

iN ONE MORE HOUR
OUR LiFE GOES SOUR
THE SKY CHEATS US
THE FiRE EATS US

WE GROW

& GROW & GROW
SO SLOW & SLOW & SLOW
ALL OF A SUDDEN WE ARE THERE
TALL & LEAN & FAT & SQUARE
ALL THE CREATURES CHECK US OUT
ALL THE CREATURES SCREAM & SHOUT
STOP THIS OVER-RATED RACE
CHECK THEM OUT & CHECK THEIR PACE
PICK & SHOVEL HOE & SHOE
GIVE THEM SOMETHING GOOD TO DO
MUSIC DANDELION SALAD
(DRUNKEN BRAWLS EQUALLY VALID)
BUT PREVENT THEIR OVERWHELMING
SELF-ENGROSSED NEVER ENDING
EMPIRESHIP OVER EVERYBODY & EVERYTHING
ALL JUDGED BY THEIR ALL-CONSUMING
LOVE OR SELF-INTEREST AMEN BYE-BYE
BE WELL DON'T OVERSTEP YOUR BOUNDERIES
FOREVER YOURS
YOURS SINCERELY

(11)

BREAD & PUPPET
PRESS 2004
GLOVER VT

BREAD & PUPPET

KASPER 10

155

4. LIFE IS IMMIGRANTS WHO ARE NEEDED BUT MUST NOT EXIST. LIFE IS AIR WHICH WANTS TO BREATHE BUT IS CONDEMNED TO STINK. LIFE IS FLOCKS OF POPULATIONS WHOSE WINGS

5. ARE BROKEN BY THE OCCUPIER. LIFE IS WINTER DEFROSTED BY THE FREEZERS OF THE OCCUPIER

6. LIFE IS WHAT WANTS TO BE BUT IT CANNOT BE BECAUSE THE DEFENSE DEPT. UNLOADS ITS BOMBS ON IT

7. LIFE IS THE GREAT BEAUTY OF THE UNIVERSE WHICH MUST BE ERADICATED BECAUSE THE PROGRAM OF THE OCCUPIER IS MODERNITY

156

⑧ MODERNITY IS A FINAL HUMAN PRODUCT
OF A SPECIFIC STYLE WHICH MUST NOT BE
DISTURBED. THE NAME OF THIS STYLE IS:
INTELLIGENCE.

⑨ INTELLIGENCE LIVES IN A PLEASANT
LIGHTLY FURNISHED APARTMENT OF GREAT
SUBSTANCE WITH PRIVATE TRANSPORTATION
SERVICE TO THE EQUALLY PLEASANT
LIGHTLY FURNISHED OFFICE OF GREAT
SUBSTANCE. BOTH ARE HEAVILY
INSURED AGAINST ALL EVIL, E.G.
WIND, WATER, SPRING & SUMMER.

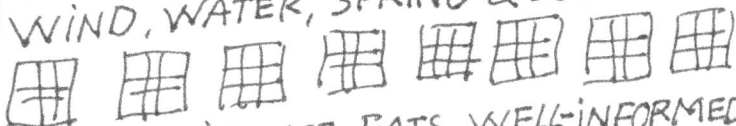

⑩ INTELLIGENCE EATS WELL-INFORMED
& SLEEPS WELL-INFORMED.

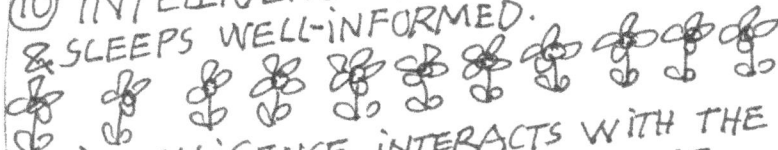

⑪ INTELLIGENCE INTERACTS WITH THE
GREAT BEAUTY OF THE UNIVERSE
DURING ITS ONE WEEK VACATION FROM
ITSELF ON THE GREAT-BEAUTY-OF-THE-
UNIVERSE RESERVATION WHICH EITHER
HAS NOT BEEN BOMBARDED
YET OR

(12) HAS BEEN SUFFICIENTLY BOMBARDED TO ALLOW FOR 2ND GREAT-BEAUTY-OF-THE-UNIVERSE GROWTH

(13) THE RESERVATIONS ARE LOCATED IN GREAT DISTANCES. THE DISTANCES ARE WELL-PREPARED FOR THE INTERACTIONS. ONLY HIGHEST VALUE COUNTRIES WITH NO UNSURMOUNTABLE DISTANCES PROVIDE THESE SERVICES

(14) THE LIFESTYLE OF INTELLIGENCE IS FINAL & CAN ONLY GET BETTER SINCE IT IS EXCLUSIVE & ITS EXCLUSIVITY PROVIDES FOR ITS CHARM

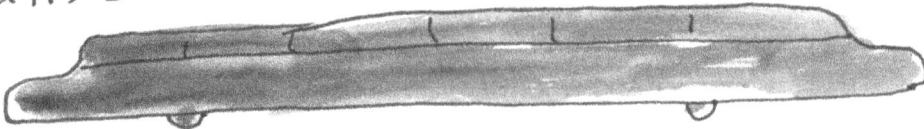

15 THE OCCUPIER'S SUCCESS IN CREATING INTELLIGENCE (AN EXCLUSIVE LIFESTYLE FOR THE BEST ONLY) REPRESENTS THE PEAK OF THE YEARNINGS OF HUMAN HISTORY & MUST BE PRESERVED BY ALL MEANS

16 THE UN-INTELLIGENT ICECOLD REALITY WHICH IS STUCK IN ANCIENT DILEMMAS & UNMUTATED SUFFERING (OUTDATED & TOTALLY UNFIT FOR MODERNITY) IS OF NO PARTICULAR INTEREST

17 & YET, KASPER, WHO LIVES IN AN ALMOST PLEASANT HEAVILY FURNISHED APARTMENT OF NO SUBSTANCE FEELS INSPIRED BY THE FOOT OF THE OCCUPIER TO RESIST ICECOLD REALITY EVEN WITHOUT THE PROPER INTELLIGENCE

WHAT IS SOUP GOOD FOR?
SOUP IS A TRICK HOW TO CORRUPT ICE COLD REALITY
YOU TAKE LITTLE BITS OF WARMTH FROM YOUR PRE-MODERN WOODSTOVE
AND YOU INFECT THE FINALITY OF THE ICE COLD SITUATION WITH THE LITTLE-BITS-OF-WARMTH VIRUS
HOORAH!
BRAVO!
BRAVISSIMO!

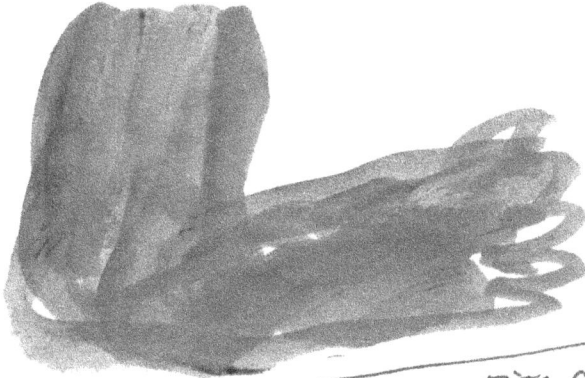

ARE THESE LITTLE BITS OF WARMTH FIGHTING MECHANISMS THAT CAN BE PROGRAMMED TO ATTACK THE FOOT?

ARE THESE LITTLE BITS OF WARMTH PACKAGEABLE FOR EXPORT TO THE 4 CORNERS OF THE ICE-COLD REALITY?

IS YOUR TRICK TRICKY ENOUGH?

DOES YOUR MOM LIKE STONE SOUP?

HOW WARM IS IT ANYWAY?

OH!

BREAD & PUPPET PRESS
2006

BREAD & PUPPET

KASPER II

KASPER'S ROOSTER

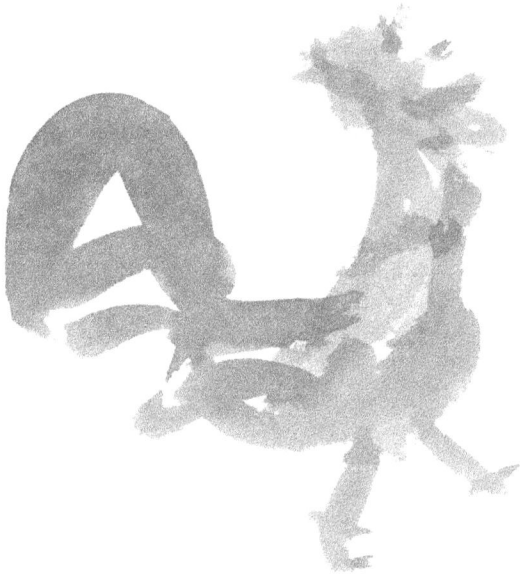

ONE DAY KASPER
FOUND A HALFDEAD
ROUSTER

AND HE BLEW
LIFE IN HIS NOSTRILS

AND THERE WAS LIFE

169

THEN HE TAUGHT
THE ROOSTER

AND THE ROOSTER

COCK A DOODLE
DOO DOO
COCK A
DOODLE

SANG

SUCCESSFULLY

AND KASPER BECAME A CHICKEN FARMER

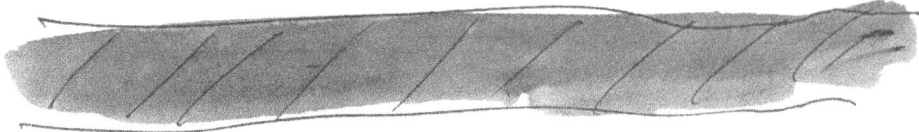

EGGS

BUT HIS SOUL PROTESTED

SO KASPER TOLD THE ROOSTER

AND HE SHREDDED THE N.Y. TIMES & FED
IT TO THE ROOSTER

AND THE ROOSTER BECAME VERY SICK
BUT HE LEARNED   1.) N.Y. TIMES ENGLISH
2.) ENGLISH 3.) CULTURAL CRITIQUE
AND WHEN HE WAS WELL AGAIN
KASPER TOOK HIM TO N.Y. CITY & PUT
HIM ON TOP OF THE EMPIRE STATE
BUILDING & ASKED HIM TO PRESENT
THE CURRENT ROOSTER PERSPECTIVE OF THE WORLD
TO THE WORLD AT LARGE (WHICH
IS A LARGE CROWD CROWDING THE
STREETS UNDERNEATH THE EMPIRE
STATE BUILDING)

WE ROOSTERS ARE HEATHENS. WE BELIEVE IN INCHWORMS & JUNEBUGS, IN GRASS PATCHES & FRESHLY HARROWED FIELDS SURROUNDED BY ROSE HEDGES OR MILKWEED & WE DON'T BELIEVE IN CRUCIFIXES OR GRAND CREATOR DADDIES BECAUSE WE ARE APOSTLES OF NOTHING WHICH IS A NOTHING FULL OF MIRACLES & OUR EYES ARE ON THE GREAT BEAUTY OF THE UNIVERSE & WE SEE THAT GOVERNMENTS ARE LAZY SELF-SERVING ENTERPRISES WHICH BELITTLE THE WORLD & WAGE WAR & DESTRUCTION ON THE GREAT BEAUTY OF THE UNIVERSE & ARE DEFINITELY NOT SERVING THE INTERESTS OF ANIMALS OR HUMANS OR MOUNTAINS OR ANY HOLY FORM OF LIFE & THEREFORE WE URGE YOU TO GET RID OF THEM & ALIGN YOURSELVES WITH MORE REASONABLE FORCES

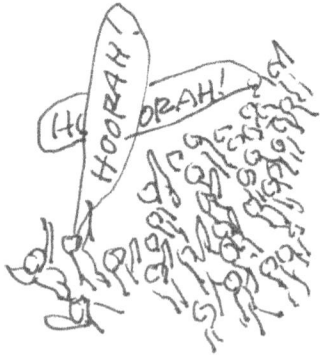

HOORAH! HOORAH!

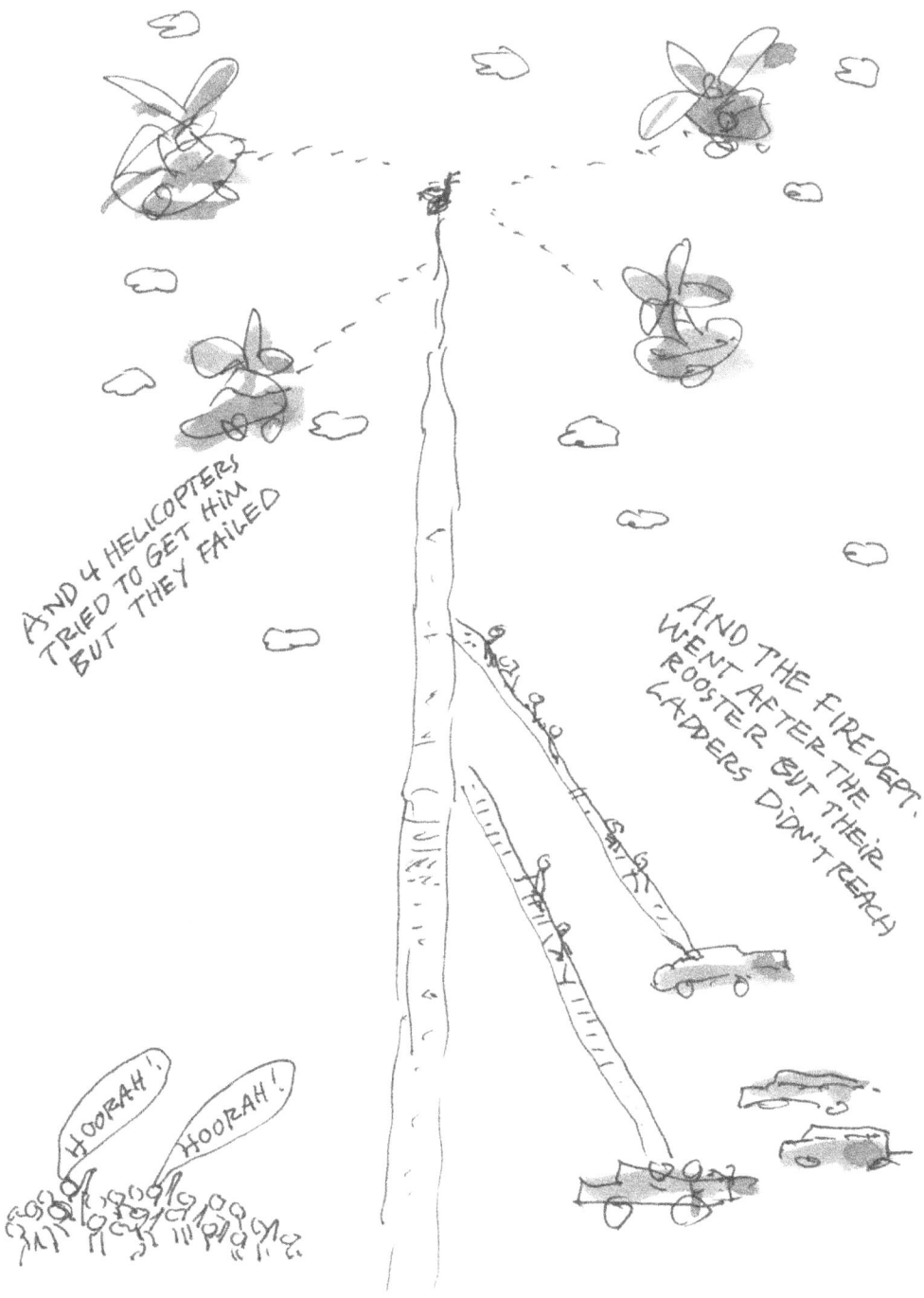

AND 4 HELICOPTERS
TRIED TO GET HIM
BUT THEY FAILED

AND THE FIRE DEPT.
WENT AFTER THE
ROOSTER BUT THEIR
LADDERS DIDN'T REACH

HOORAH!
HOORAH!

& THE ROOSTER DIDN'T STOP TALKING

THERE IS AN ESTABLISHED WORLD INSTRUCTED BY THE LATEST INTELLIGENCE THAT KNOWS EXACTLY HOW TO DO THINGS. E.G. ART, THEATRE, COMMUNICATION. ALL THESE ARE PART OF MODERNITY WHICH IS A HAPPY TECHNO-BUROCRACY FOR THE WEALTHY & THE UNWEALTHY WHO DON'T REALIZE THEY ARE WEALTHY. BUT WE ROOSTERS SAY: RADICAL ART IS INSTRUCTED BY THE UNKNOWN. THE GOVERNMENTS WHICH MUST BE GOTTEN RID OF CAN ONLY BE GOTTEN RID OF BY THE EMPLOYMENT OF UNKNOWNS. THE EXISTING ARTS & CRAFTS & INTELLIGENCE HAVE FAILED TO OVERTHROW THEM. ONLY THE RADICAL ARTS OF UNKNOWNS CAN INVENT THE POETRY WHICH WILL EXPOSE THE IRREALITY OF THE RULING LANGUAGE. ONLY THE RADICAL PAINTING OF THE UNKNOWNS CAN TOPPLE THE HIERARCHY OF THE PICTURES WHICH EDUCATE THE MASSES. ONLY THE ANTI-FEAR DANCERS CAN TACKLE THE HYPE OF INSTITUTIONALIZED FEAR

BREAD & PUPPET
PRESS 2006
GLOVER VT

180

BREAD & PUPPET

KASPER 12

KASPER TAKES A SOCIOLOGY CLASS AT THE HEART-OF-SOCIETY INSTITUTE

HEART-OF-
SOCIETY
INSTITUTE

IS LOCATED IN THE HEART OF THE CITY.
24 HRS SERVICE. BOTH HUMAN + INHUMAN
RESOURCES ADMINISTRATORS ADDRESS BASIC
+ RANDOM QUESTIONS CONCERNING THE HEART
OF SOCIETY. NO DOGS ALLOWED. NO FOOD OR DRINK.
(NO PERFUME OR STINK). EVER SINCE THE HEART
OF SOCIETY SUFFERED A HEART ATTACK STUDENTS
ARE SCREENED NOT ONLY PHYSICALLY BUT PSYCHOLOGI-
CALLY AS WELL TO PREVENT ANY AGGRESSIVE
THOUGHT OR ACTION THAT MIGHT AFFLICT
THE ALREADY DELICATE CONDITION OF THE
HEART OF SOCIETY

THE 3-STRIKE-OUT PHENOMENON HAS TO BE CREDITED TO THE HUMAN RESOURCES DISTRIBUTORS WHOSE TASK IS TO DISTRIBUTE HUMAN RESOURCES AS EFFECTIVELY AS POSSIBLE TO THE PRODUCTIVE SOCIETY. SOCIETY IS DIVIDED INTO 2 DISTINCT CATEGORIES. CATEGORY A IS THE PRODUCTIVE SOCIETY WHICH IS THE DRESSED-UP SOCIETY WHOSE APPEARANCE REFLECTS ITS PRODUCTIVE ASPIRATIONS. CATEGORY B IS THE UNPRODUCTIVE OR NAKED SOCIETY WHICH EXISTS AS SUBVERSIVE FORCE INSIDE THE DRESSED UP SOCIETY + MUST BE KEPT IN SUBMISSION IF PRODUCTION IS TO BE ACHIEVED

WHAT?

THE 3-STRIKE-OUT POLICY IS A MAJOR ACCOMPLISHMENT OF THE HUMAN RESOURCES DISTRIBUTORS ARDUOUS EFFORTS TO CONTAIN THE NAKED POPULATION TENDENCIES WHICH ENDANGER PRODUCTION. THE NAKED SOCIETY WHICH REPRESENTS THE ILL WILL INSIDE THE GOOD WILL OF THE DRESSED-UP SOCIETY IS THE BREEDING GROUND OF THE REPEAT OFFENDERS WHOM THE 3-STRIKE POLICY ADDRESSES.

MY DAD ALWAYS SAID: "STRIKE IT ONCE, STRIKE IT TWICE, STRIKE IT THRICE."

187

HUMAN RESOURCES DISTRIBUTORS ATTEMPT TO CHANNEL OFFENDERS INTO THE CORRECT PRICE CATEGORY OF THE CORRECTIVE PROCESS. BY COMPARING THE PRICETAGS OF 2 ALTERNATIVELY SITUATED VENUES OF CORRECTIVE INSTITUTIONALIZATION THEY ARRIVE AT THE OBVIOUS CHOICE. VENUE 1 IS HARVARD COLLEGE, AT $50.000 PER YEAR. VENUE 2 IS PRISON, AT $60.000 PER YEAR, AN OBVIOUSLY SUPERIOR SERVICE.

WHAT YARDSTICK DO YOU USE?

GOOD IS EXPENSIVE. BAD IS CHEAP. PROBLEMS ARE CHEAP. SOLUTIONS ARE EXPENSIVE OUR SPECIALTY IS SOLUTIONS. BESIDES EVERYBODY KNOWS! GOOD IS ONLY GOOD BECAUSE IT IS EXPENSIVE. EXPENSIVE IS GOOD + THEREFORE IT IS MAGNIFICENT + THEREFORE IT IS DIVINE

AT THAT POINT KASPER WHO HAD
CONSUMED A TERRIFIC HELPING OF HIS
FAVORITE BREAKFAST : BEANSOUP
COULD CONTAIN HIMSELF NO LONGER

AND THE HEART OF SOCIETY
DIED THE HEART-ATTACK-DEATH .
AND THE QUESTION AROSE : HOW
CAN SOCIETY SURVIVE WITHOUT
A HEART ?

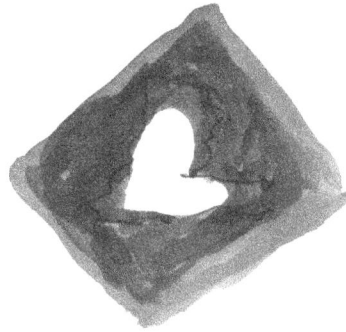

BREAD&PUPPET
PRESS 2006
GLOVER VT

BREAD & PUPPET

KASPER 13

LOVE

WHEN KASPER WAS 100 YEARS OLD & DECREPIT

A FLY TICKLED HIS NOSE

AND WITH THE HELP OF A FLY-SQUATTER

KASPER KILLED THE FLY

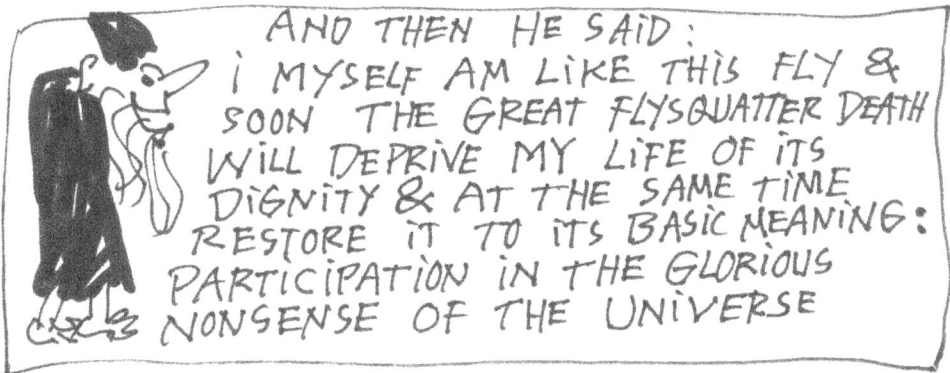

AND THEN HE SAID: i MYSELF AM LiKE THiS FLY & SOON THE GREAT FLYSQUATTER DEATH WiLL DEPRIVE MY LiFE OF iTS DiGNiTY & AT THE SAME TiME RESTORE iT TO iTS BASiC MEANING: PARTICIPATION IN THE GLORIOUS NONSENSE OF THE UNIVERSE

& IN ANTICIPATION OF THE GLORIOUS NONSENSE OF THE UNIVERSE I MUST NOW PRACTICE MY OWN NONSENSE.

& THEN KASPER WHO WAS 100 YEARS OLD & DECREPIT DID NOT SUCCEED TO WATCH HIS OWN STEP AND HE

FELL OVER BEAUTIFUL YOUNG LADY

AND HE FELL IN LOVE WITH HER

WITH HER

WHO WAS A REPRESENTATIVE OF THE GODDESS OF LOVE APHRODITE BORN IRRESISTIBLE & ALSO NOT SHY

& KASPER

SANG LIKE A BIRD

& HE SANG THE FAMOUS LOVESONG:

I WANT TO HOLD YOUR FOOT

FOO-OO-OO-OO-OO-T

& THE REPRESENTA-TIVE OF THE GODDESS APHRODITE WAS SO DELIGHTED

SHE TURNED INTO A HORSE

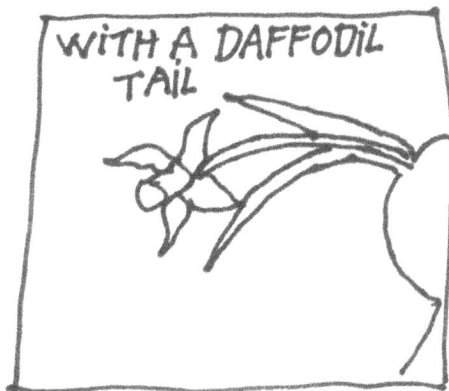

WITH A DAFFODIL TAIL

& THE SUN SHINING OUT OF ITS NOSTRILS

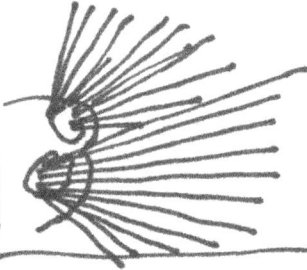

& KASPER JUMPED ON THE HORSE

& RODE THE HORSE

UPHILL

AND

DOWNHILL

& LEFT

& RIGHT

& THIS WAY

& THAT WAY

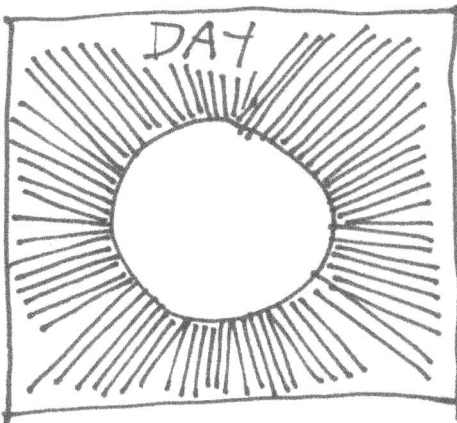

DAY

& NIGHT

THROUGH THUNDER

& LIGHTNING

TILL

THE WEATHER CHANGED

& THE CLOUDS

LOOKED

UGLY

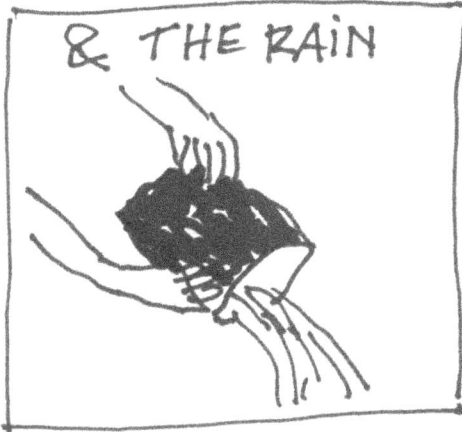

& THE RAIN

CAME POURING DOWN

& THE HORSE BECAME A MUDPUDDLE

& THE HORSE'S TAIL BECAME A DAFFODIL FOREST

204

BUT HE COULDN'T
FIND HER

& HE WENT HOME

& HE SCRATCHED HIS
NOSE WITH THE
FLY SQUATTER

& HE KISSED THE
MOON GOOD NIGHT

& HE SANK

INTO OBLIVION

BREAD & PUPPET
PRESS 2006
GLOVER VT.

208

BREAD & PUPPET

KASPER 14

THE LIGHTBULB TRAGEDY

OR WHAT ARE OUR LIGHTBULBS AND HOW DO THEY ENLIGHTEN US

KASPER LIVES IN THE VICINITY OF A

LIGHTBULB

A VERY TOUGH

& AGGRESSIVE LIGHT BULB

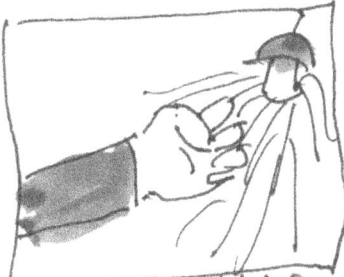

& KASPER HAS ENOUGH

& HE SMASHES THE LIGHTBULB

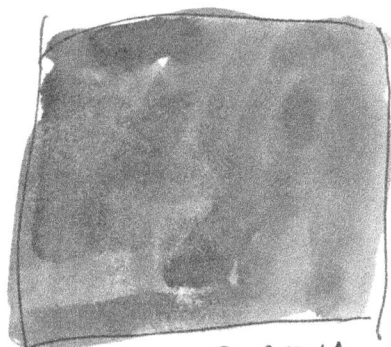

& IN THE DARK
HE LEARNS ALL ABOUT
DARKNESS

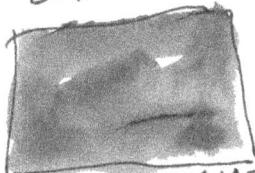

DARKNESS IS
ENORMOUS

YOU CAN'T MAKE OUT
THE DIFFERENCE
BETWEEN THE
BEGINNING & THE END

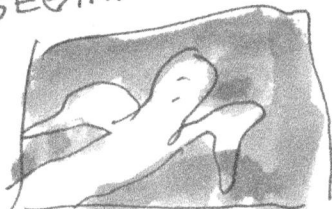

DEATH LOOKS
ALMOST THE SAME
AS LIFE

THE WORLD IS RUN
BY MYSTERIES

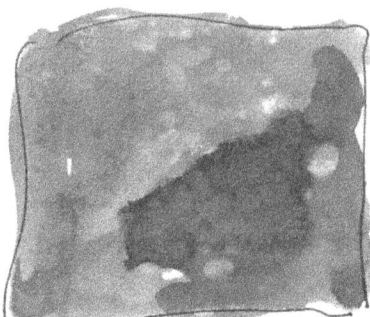

PEOPLE FALL ALL
THE TIME &
THEREFORE THINGS
KEEP BREAKING

AND PEOPLE FALL

& FALL

& FALL

& THINGS BREAK

& BREAK

TILL THE LIGHTBULB
GETS INVENTED

213

ONLY WHEN THE LIGHTBULB GETS INVENTED

IS HUMANITY ENLIGHTENED

A

A LITTLE BIT

B

A LOT

C

TREMENDOUSLY

& THIS TREMENDOUS ENLIGHTENMENT HAS 2 RESULTS:

THE LIGHTBULB RELIGION (COMPLETE WITH LIGHTBULB MESSIA WHO HAS TO BE SACRIFICED)

①

& THE LIGHTBULB REPUBLIC

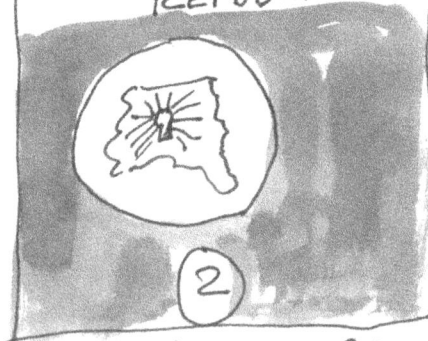

②

(THE DARK ONES GO UNDERGROUND)

WHAT'S NEXT?

NEXT

ARE THE LIGHT-
BULB WARS

WHICH WAGE WAR
AGAINST ALL PARTS
UN-ENLIGHTENED

WITH THE OBJECTIVE
TO EXPORT

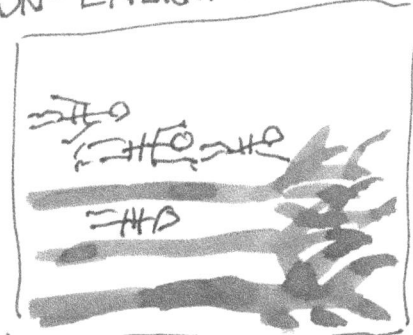

THE LIGHT BULB CULTURE
TO THE MOST DISTANT REGIONS

215

WHAT DO THEY GET OUT OF IT?

AS COMPENSATION FOR BEING DESTROYED

THE MOST DISTANT REGIONS

GET HOSPITALS FOR THE SURVIVORS

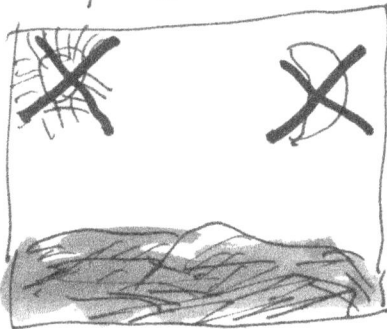

AND

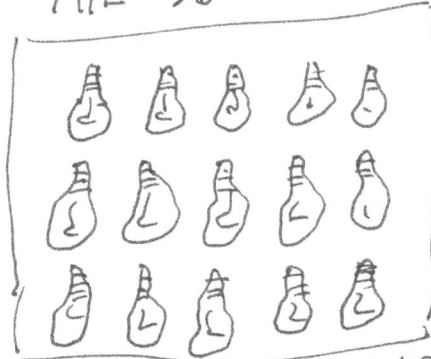

AN ENORMOUS LIGHTBULB ECONOMY

WHAT ELSE?

RELIGION

THE LIGHTBULB MISSIONARIES

AN ESSENTIAL PART OF THE CULTURAL EXPORT

SEE TO IT THAT THE UN-ENLIGHTENED MASSES

GET THE PROPER APPRECIATION OF LIGHTBULBS + THEIR SPIRITUAL POTENTIALS

AND?

IN ORDER TO IMPLEMENT THE

LIGHTBULB LAWS, AS
PRESCRIBED BY THE
ENLIGHTENED SCIENCES

A SPECIAL LIGHTBULB TASK FORCE

INSTILLS TOTAL LIGHTBULB
DESIRABILITY

IN THE POPULATION

& ANIMALS WHO USED
TO BE HUMAN ARE
RECLASSIFIED & ALOTTED
THEIR SPECIES-SPECIFIC
QUANTITIES OF LIGHTBULB
LIGHT

220

BREAD & PUPPET
PRESS 2006

BREAD & PUPPET

KASPER 14 A

THE LIGHTBULB TRAGEDY ANNEX

KASPER TRIES

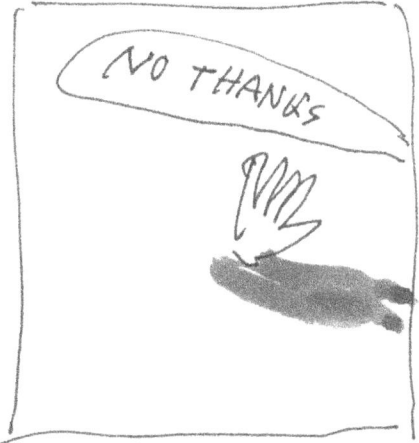

WITH THE HELP OF HIS LIGHTBULB

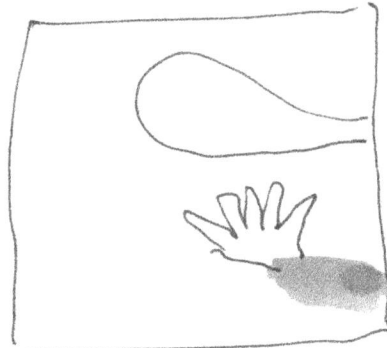

MY LIFE AS A LIGHTBULB

EVEN THOUGH I AM NOT FOND OF THE FAMOUS ELECTRICITY WHICH ENNOBLES OUR LIFE MY LIFE IS CONDEMNED TO LIGHTBULB STATUS

HOW ELSE CAN I UNDERSTAND THIS CONTINUOUS ON & OFF SWITCHING OF TINY PARTICLES OF LIGHT WHICH ISSUE FROM MY WORKSHOP IN ALL DIRECTIONS?

AND WHAT IF NOT LIGHTBULB POWER CHECKS THE FRIGHTFUL DARKNESS OF SOLOISTS?

LIKE THE LIGHTBULB MY PRODUCTION HANGS FROM THE CEILING ABOVE THE COUCH OF MY FELLOW CITIZENS & GETS TURNED OFF LIKE A LIGHTBULB

i MUST i MUST i MUST

THE LIGHTBULB
QUESTIONS OF LIFE

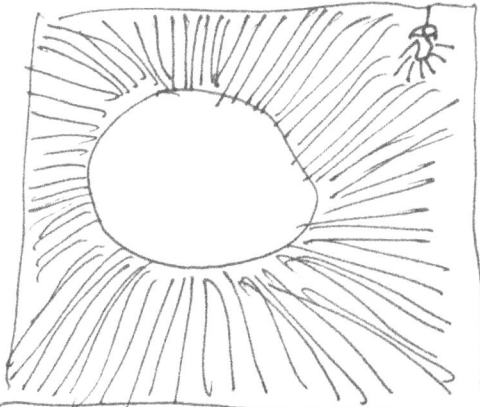

ARE THE LIGHTBULBS SUN IMITATIONS TRYING TO BRING THE DEAR SUNLIGHT INTO OUR MESSY KITCHEN

& BY DOING SO PUNISHING US WITH OUR OWN MESSINESS?

OR ARE THESE LIGHTBULBS POSSESSED BY THE EVIL SPIRIT

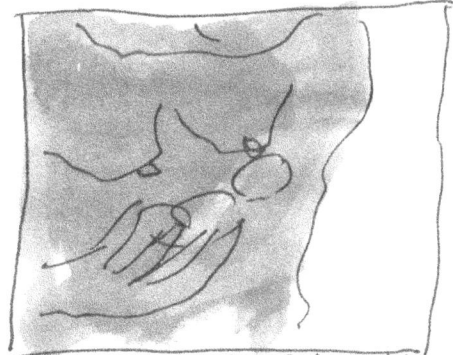

& WANT TO DEPRIVE US OF THE NATURAL DARKNESS WHICH HAS NURSED US SO LONG?

232

OH MY LIGHTBULB WHY DO YOU
ABANDON ME? i WAKE UP IN THE
MIDDLE OF THE
NIGHT IN GREAT
DISTRESS.
MY LAZY LIMBS
YEARN FOR
HAPPINESS
BUT MY
LIGHTBULB
WAKES ME &
BOTHERS ME
& DENIES THE
NIGHT & SITS
ON MY BRAIN &
FEEDS ME 1000 COMPLAINTS ABOUT
ALL THE UNFINISHEDNESS & THE
LIGHTBULB CHEATS ME BECAUSE IT
DOES NOT PENETRATE THE SKULL & THE
COMPLAINTS FESTER LIKE BUGBITES AND
AND AND AND

AND AND

AND

WHEN I AM THE SUN, I GET UP
VERY EARLY BEFORE THE COFFEE &
IN THE EVENING I SET LIKE THE SUN IN
THE DARK & I LOVE THE WIND & THE BREASTS
& THIGHS OF LOVE & THE ROOF OF THE HOUSE
THAT PROTECTS ME FROM THE RAIN. THE
GREAT UNIVERSE PAINTS THE STARRY SKY.
THE WIND LISTENS WHEN I PRAISE THE STARS
& THE BLACK CLOUDS, THE DRUNKARDS,
INVADING THE HORIZON & THE TIN SHOT GLASS
THAT TREATS ME SO NICE.

234

BREAD & PUPPET
PRESS 2006

Fomite
Burlington, Vermont

Fomite is a literary press whose authors and artists explore the human condition -- political, cultural, personal and historical -- in poetry and prose.

A fomite is a medium capable of transmitting infectious organisms from one individual to another.

"The activity of art is based on the capacity of people to be infected by the feelings of others." Tolstoy, *What is Art?*

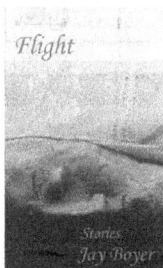

Flight and Other Stories - Jay Boyer

In *Flight and Other Stories,* we're with the fattest woman on earth as she draws her last breaths and her soul ascends toward its final reward. We meet a divorcee who can fly for no more effort than flapping her arms. We follow a middle-aged butler whose love affair with a young woman leads him first to the mysteries of bondage, and then to the pleasures of malice. Story by story, we set foot into worlds so strange as to seem all but surreal, yet everything feels familiar, each moment rings true. And that's when we recognize we're in the hands of one of America's truly original talents.

AlphaBetaBestiario - Antonello Borra

Animals have always understood that mankind is not fully at home in the world. Bestiaries, hoping to teach, send out warnings. This one, of course, aims at doing the same.

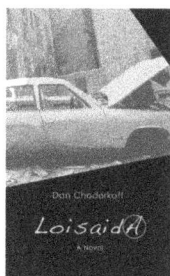

Loisaida - Dan Chodorokoff

Catherine, a young anarchist estranged from her parents and squatting in an abandoned building on New York's Lower East Side is fighting with her boyfriend and conflicted about her work on an underground newspaper. After learning of a developer's plans to demolish a community garden, Catherine builds an alliance with a group of Puerto Rican community activists. Together they confront the confluence of politics, money, and real estate that rule Manhattan. All the while she learns important lessons from her great-grandmother's life in the Yiddish anarchist movement that flourished on the Lower East Side at the turn of the century. In this coming of age story, family saga, and tale of urban politics, Dan Chodorkoff explores the "principle of hope", and examines how memory and imagination inform social change.

Fomite
Burlington, Vermont

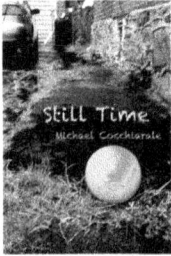

Still Time - Michael Cocchiarale

Still Time is a collection of twenty-five short and shorter stories exploring tensions that arise in a variety of contemporary relationships: a young boy must deal with the wrath of his out-of-work father; a woman runs into a man twenty years after an awkward sexual encounter; a wife, unable to conceive, imagines her own murder, as well as the reaction of her emotionally distant husband; a soon-to-be tenured English professor tries to come to terms with her husband's shocking return to the religion of his youth; an assembly line worker, married for thirty years, discovers the surprising secret life of his recently hospitalized wife. Whether a few hundred or a few thousand words, these and other stories in the collection depict characters at moments of deep crisis. Some feel powerless, overwhelmed—unable to do much to change the course of their lives. Others rise to the occasion and, for better or for worse, say or do the thing that might transform them for good. Even in stories with the most troubling of endings, there remains the possibility of redemption. For each of the characters, there is still time.

❧ ❧ ❧

Improvisational Arguments - Anna Faktorovich

Improvisational Arguments is written in free verse to capture the essence of modern problems and triumphs. The poems clearly relate short, frequently humorous and occasionally tragic, stories about travels to exotic and unusual places, fantastic realms, abnormal jobs, artistic innovations, political objections, and misadventures with love.

❧ ❧ ❧

The Listener Aspires to the Condition of Music - Barry Goldensohn

"I know of no other selected poems that selects on one theme, but this one does, charting Goldensohn's career-long attraction to music's performance, consolations and its august, thrilling, scary and clownish charms. Does all art aspire to the condition of music as Pater claimed, exhaling in a swoon toward that one class act? Goldensohn is more aware than the late 19th century of the overtones of such breathing: his poems thoroughly round out those overtones in a poet's lifetime of listening."
John Peck, poet, editor, Fellow of the American Academy of Rome

❧ ❧ ❧

Fomite
Burlington, Vermont

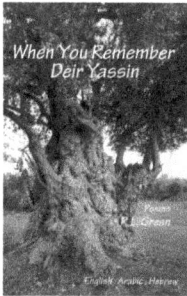

When You Remember Deir Yassin - R.L Green

When You Remember Deir Yassin is a collection of poems by R. L. Green, an American Jewish writer, on the subject of the occupation and destruction of Palestine. Green comments: "Outspoken Jewish critics of Israeli crimes against humanity have, strangely, been called "anti-Semitic" as well as the hilariously illogical epithet "self-hating Jews." As a Jewish critic of the Israeli government, I have come to accept these accusations as a stamp of approval and a badge of honor, signifying my own fealty to a central element of Jewish identity and ethics: one must be a lover of truth and a friend to the oppressed, and stand with the victims of tyranny, not with the tyrants, despite tribal loyalty or self-advancement. These poems were written as expressions of outrage, and of grief, and to encourage my sisters and brothers of every cultural or national grouping to speak out against injustice, to try to save Palestine, and in so doing, to reclaim for myself my own place as part of the Jewish people." The poems are offered in the original English with Arabic and Hebrew translations accompanying each poem.

❧ ❧ ❧

The Co-Conspirator's Tale - Ron Jacobs

There's a place where love and mistrust are never at peace; where duplicity and deceit are the universal currency. *The Co-Conspirator's Tale* takes place within this nebulous firmament. There are crimes committed by the police in the name of the law. Excess in the name of revolution. The combination leaves death in its wake and the survivors struggling to find justice in a San Francisco Bay Area noir by the author of the underground classic *The Way the Wind Blew: A History of the Weather Underground* and the novel *Short Order Frame Up*.

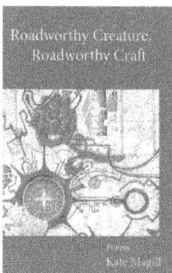

❧ ❧ ❧

Roadworthy Creature, Roadworthy Craft - Kate Magill

Words fail but the voice struggles on. The culmination of a decade's worth of performance poetry, *Roadworthy Creature, Roadworthy Craft* is Kate Magill's first full-length publication. In lines that are sinewy yet delicate, Magill's poems explore the terrain where idea and action meet, where bodies and words commingle to form a strange new flesh, a breathing text, an "I" that spirals outward from itself.

Fomite
Burlington, Vermont

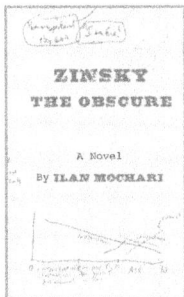

Zinsky the Obscure - Ilan Mochari

"If your childhood is brutal, your adulthood becomes a daily attempt to recover: a quest for ecstasy and stability in recompense for their early absence." So states the 30-year-old Ariel Zinsky, whose bachelor-like lifestyle belies the torturous youth he is still coming to grips with. As a boy, he struggles with the beatings themselves; as a grownup, he struggles with the world's indifference to them. *Zinsky the Obscure* is his life story, a humorous chronicle of his search for a redemptive ecstasy through sex, an entrepreneurial sports obsession, and finally, the cathartic exercise of writing it all down. Fervently recounting both the comic delights and the frightening horrors of a life in which he feels – always – that he is not like all the rest, Zinsky survives the worst and relishes the best with idiosyncratic style, as his heartbreak turns into self-awareness and his suicidal ideation into self-regard. A vivid evocation of the all-consuming nature of lust and ambition – and the forces that drive them – *Zinsky the Obscure* is a novel of extraordinary zeal, range, and power.

❧ ❧ ❧

The Derivation of Cowboys & Indians - Joseph D. Reich

The Derivation of Cowboys & Indians represents a profound journey, a breakdown of The American Dream from a social, cultural, historical, and spiritual point of view. Reich examines in concise!detail the loss of the collective unconscious, commenting on our!contemporary postmodern culture with its self-interested excesses, on where and how things all go wrong, and how social/political practice rarely meets its original proclamations and promises. Reich's surreal and self-effacing satire brings this troubling message home. *The Derivations of Cowboys & Indians* is a desperate search and struggle for America's literal, symbolic, and spiritual home.

❧ ❧ ❧

Kasper Planet: Comix and Tragix - Peter Schumann

The British call him Punch, the Italians, Pulchinello, the Russians, Petruchka, the Native Americans, Coyote. These are the figures we may know. But every culture that worships authority will breed a Punch-like, anti-authoritan resister. Yin and yang -- it has to happen. The Germans call him Kasper. Truth-telling and serious pranking are dangerous professions when going up against power. Bradley Manning sits naked in solitary; Julian Assange is pursued by Interpol, Obama's Department of Justice, and Amazon.com. But -- in contrast to merely human faces -- masks and theater can often slip through the bars. Consider our American Kaspers: Charlie Chaplin, Woody Guthrie, Abby Hoffman, the Yes Men -- theater people all, utilizing various forms to seed critique. Their profiles and tactics have evolved along with those of their enemies.

Who are the bad guys that call forth the Kaspers? Over the last half century, with his Bread & Puppet Theater, Peter Schumann has been tireless in naming them, excoriating them with Kasperdom....

from Marc Estrin's Foreword to Planet Kasper

Fomite
Burlington, Vermont

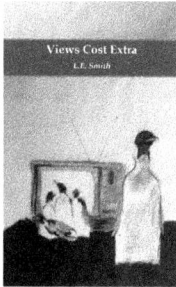

Views Cost Extra - L.E. Smith

Views that inspire, that calm, or that terrify – all come at some cost to the viewer. In *Views Cost Extra* you will find a New Jersey high school preppy who wants to inhabit the "perfect" cowboy movie, a rural mailman disgusted with the residents of his town who wants to live with the penguins, an ailing screen writer who strikes a deal with Johnny Cash to reverse an old man's failures, an old man who ponders a young man's suicide attempt, a one-armed blind blues singer who wants to reunite with the car that took her arm on the assembly line -- and more. These stories suggest that we must pay something to live even ordinary lives.

The Empty Notebook Interrogates Itself - Susan Thomas

The Empty Notebook began its life as a very literal metaphor for a few weeks of what the poet thought was writer's block, but was really the struggle of an eccentric persona to take over her working life. It won. And for the next three years everything she wrote came to her in the voice of the Empty Notebook, who, as the notebook began to fill itself, became rather opinionated, changed gender, alternately acted as bully and victim, had many bizarre adventures in exotic locales and developed a somewhat politically-incorrect attitude. It then began to steal the voices and forms of other poets and tried to immortalize itself in various poetry reviews. It is now thrilled to collect itself in one slim volume.

My God, What Have We Done? - Susan Weiss

In a world afflicted with war, toxicity, and hunger, does what we do in our private lives really matter? Fifty years after the creation of the atomic bomb at Los Alamos, newlyweds Pauline and Clifford visit that once-secret city on their honeymoon, compelled by Pauline's fascination with Oppenheimer, the soulful scientist. The two stories emerging from this visit reverberate back and forth between the loneliness of a new mother at home in Boston and the isolation of an entire community dedicated to the development of the bomb. While Pauline struggles with unforeseen challenges of family life, Oppenheimer and his crew reckon with forces beyond all imagining.

Finally the years of frantic research on the bomb culminate in a stunning test explosion that echoes a rupture in the couple's marriage. Against the backdrop of a civilization that's out of control, Pauline begins to understand the complex, potentially explosive physics of personal relationships.

At once funny and dead serious, *My God, What Have We Done?* sifts through the ruins left by the bomb in search of a more worthy human achievement.

www.ingramcontent.com/pod-product-compliance
Lightning Source LLC
Chambersburg PA
CBHW080247030426
42334CB00023BA/2726